Grandma,
Tell Me a Story...

About Critters

Grandma, Tell Me a Story...

About Critters

Lynn Ransford

Illustrations by the Author

Book Two in the
Grandma, Tell Me a Story Series

Lucky Valley Press
2022

Grandma, Tell Me a Story...About Critters

Copyright © 2022 Lynn Ransford

All rights reserved

Illustrations by the author

This is Book Two in the
Grandma, Tell Me a Story Series

ISBN: 9780578296524

Designed and Published by
Lucky Valley Press
Jacksonville, Oregon
luckyvalleypress.com

Contact: info@luckyvalleypress.com

Cover photo: photographybyjw/shutterstock.com

5/2022

Contents

Introduction and Dedication

I've always been surrounded by critters–most of them welcomed, some not so much (like the rattlesnake on my sleeping bag or the hungry little field mouse in Mexico). Over the years, my grandchildren have asked repeatedly for scary, silly, or touching stories of snakes and wild rats, or remarkable tales of "Ted the Toad." Some of these stories have become part of family tradition: sitting around at holiday times, taking turns sharing indelible memories, laughing hysterically. This book was written to share some of that fun with you, my readers.

I was born into a city home with dogs and cats. When my family moved to a chicken ranch, with the cats and dogs, we acquired hundreds of chickens, two geese, some rabbits, more dogs and cats, a horse, and zillions of guppies. I had fish bowls and jars all around my room, so I could watch my pregnant mama guppies give live birth to miniscule babies. I kept jars with caterpillars. I fed them leaves, kept the cocoons, and watched spellbound as butterflies emerged and unfolded–spectacular!

Later, I began raising crickets to feed the various lizards and toads my brothers and I captured. And still later, I had generations of mealworms living in a shoebox for the occasional reptile or amphibians my sons brought home.

As a schoolteacher, my menagerie grew. I believed animals in the classroom were important for teaching life science and also for social-emotional learning: care and responsibility for others, gentleness and kindness, and acceptance of death as part of the life cycle.

Animals in the classroom provided memorable experiences and made education alive and fun for all of us.

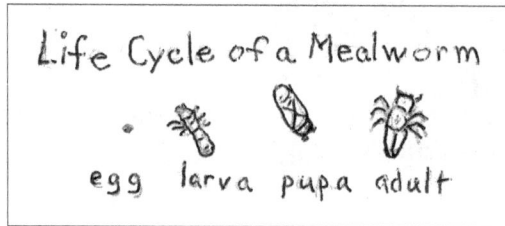

Just a note here: about "alive." One of my most horrifying teaching experiences, one I've never forgotten, occurred when I was a kindergarten teacher in the Ocean View School District in Huntington Beach, California. A fourth grader came into my classroom, tears in his eyes, begging me to adopt his pet lizard. His parents said he couldn't keep it at home. I told him I would be glad to have his lizard but asked, "Are you sure your teacher wouldn't like a lizard in your class—as part of Westward Movement and desert studies?"

"No," he nearly sobbed, "My teacher said 'nothing living in our classroom'." I stifled a gasp. Did that teacher know what she said? ..."Nothing living" in her class? How deadly was that remark? I assured the 4th grade boy that he could come to my classroom to visit his pet lizard any time.

I was more determined than ever that my classroom would always be alive–full of life for all kinds of critters. That pledge was part of my personal public school challenge: I was going to do my best to make public school every bit as enjoyable as pre-school. For years, graduates from my nursery school settings returned for visits saying they wished they were back in pre-school! Yikes!

What was wrong with public schools? I went off to K-12 teaching with the goal of making traditional school years just as alive and valued as preschool. Critters (and lots of art projects) helped me achieve that goal.

I'm still in touch with a number of my students (now parents themselves) from the Ocean View and Cypress School Districts in southern California, who fondly remember Queenie the King Snake, our happy chirping crickets, the amusing stink bugs, the lovable squeaking guinea pig.... My students, my grandchildren, and adult family members still enjoy the re-telling of those critter stories. I've included some of the favorites here.

These stories are dedicated to my grandchildren, the eager listeners who encouraged me, again and again, to "tell me a story." I hope that hidden in the stories are numerous family values: appreciation and care for one another, enjoyment of life, curiosity, education, sharing, adventure, humor…"Critter" stories are part of my memoirs – I hope to preserve family events and give something of myself, and my love, to my children and grandchildren…and you.

1

My Friend Willy May Have Saved My Life

When I was ten, I faced grave danger. I wasn't even aware of it until it was all over. It happened on my first Girl Scout camping trip, to Camp Pajarito, in the mountains near Los Angeles.

Milly, our leader, (Willy's mom) and her assistant leader, Cookie Slusser's mom, whom we called "Shrimp," prepared us for the campout. They taught us to make "sit-upons," pocket stew, bedrolls, and how to wrap ground meat, potatoes, and carrots in tin foil to cook in the fire. We already knew how to make s'mores.[1] We slept on the ground, in our blankets, under the stars, no tents.

The first morning my best friend Willy awakened me gently.[2] Willy whispered to me, "Don't move. Whatever you do, don't move."

I opened one eye to see Willy hovering nearby, the other girls behind her, wide-eyed and frightened-looking.

"Don't move," Willy calmly continued to repeat.

She said, "If you hold still, it will just go away and not hurt you."

She was insistent: "You can't move."

---

1   In case you don't know about s'mores: you toast a marshmallow over a campfire, squish it between two graham crackers with a square of chocolate candy bar in between. They're so good you always want "s'more!"

2   Willy was my best friend, but I was her second best friend. Previously, Willy had explained to me carefully that she had already promised Laura Riddle that she would be her best friend.

Confused, not knowing what was going on, I followed Willy's directions.

Very slowly, I became aware of a slight weight on my chest and then a slight movement. Looking down, only eyeballs moving, not moving my head, I saw the source of concern. A snake had curled up on my chest, probably for warmth. Possibly with all the girls nearby, possibly because the sun had come up, it evidently decided to leave and was uncoiling inch-by-inch and crawling off my chest. It slithered away into the bushes, but not before I saw the rattles on its tail and realized that it was a rattlesnake that had been on my chest, inches from my bare face! Willy's calm, but unquestionably stern commands to "be still" may have saved my life.

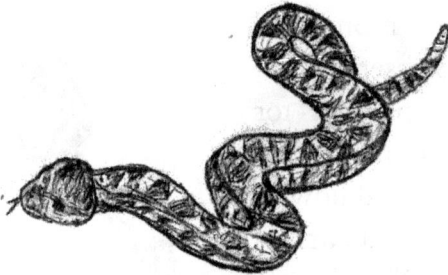

After the rattlesnake incident, we went on to have a hilarious time at Camp Pajarito. Mosquito bites were the most serious issues to address. We didn't see any other wildlife...probably because all our shrieking, giggling antics made us the wildest creatures around in and around camp![3]

---

3 Postscript: Years later, Wiily and I went off to college, to UC Santa Barbara. We kept in touch sporadically after that, until we both married "mountain men." Then the four of us hiked and camped together. Willy died in her 70s (of natural causes, not a snake bite.) In our 80s now, my husband, Jack, and Willy's husband, Pete, and I remain close, still sharing adventures.

2

Saving Secret The Snake

When I became Director of Hollywood Presbyterian Pre-School, I was fortunate to inherit a large, sunny, yellow Sunday school room with big high windows on two sides. There was plenty of room for a sand table, a dramatic play corner, a block area, and easels...an ideal early childhood setting.

I had puzzles, games, and books. But I also needed animals and science equipment. Thankfully, I was given a generous budget to purchase nearly everything on my list.

To the pet store I went. I bought a gerbil and a cage.[4] I purchased fish and a bowl. I bought an ant farm, which would allow students to observe insects working together to maintain a colony.[5] I added a microscope, magnifying glasses, a balancing scale, small weights, and various containers. But I needed a snake.

Snakes are clean and quiet, they help students overcome fears and prejudices toward living creatures that some people don't care for. Snakes, and their large terrariums, with secure lids, are expensive—not in my budget.

---

4   Gerbils are small rodents, similar to hamsters, but they don't bite. They are highly active, entertaining and sociable during the day. They can shred a toilet paper roll in minutes!

5   It was *Uncle Milton's Ant Farm*—still available today! The product has been around for over 60 years!

"But, Lady, we do have a brand-new batch of newly-born boa constrictors. Because they are so small and not guaranteed to survive, they are only $10 each," the salesman offered. I agreed to look. Oh my.

Only as big around as a pencil and about a foot long, all had clear, alert little faces: round black shiny eyes and the sweet-smile markings that seem to be permanently painted on every boa. I picked out the fattest baby boa, and an affordable plastic terrarium (which I knew I'd have to replace many times as the snake grew).

I kept the snake at home so I could observe his development through infancy. He was too tiny and fragile to be handled by preschoolers. However, I did tell my students about the snake. They couldn't understand why I didn't bring him to class, "just to look at." "Why are you keeping him secret?" they wanted to know. "Hey," one bright child piped up, "Sssecret...sss...like a sssnake...get it?" So the baby boa was named "Secret."

All went well. Every week or so, Secret ate a small "pinkie" mouse (so young it had no fur yet, just pink skin). Secret grew to be big around as my finger. And then one day, he sneezed. *Uh-oh, was that a bubble of mucus protruding from one of his nostrils?* And then he ignored the pinky mouse in his cage. Secret stopped eating. I called the pet store. "Yes...sorry...we understand...no, we can't offer any help...Wait a minute...here's the phone number of our herpetologist."

I called the herpetologist. (I could not afford an office visit for the little boa.) The herpetologist was very kind to take the time to explain: "Snakes have poor respiratory systems. They do have two lungs but often one is less developed than the other. Some snakes actually just have one lung. A snake's lungs have to be very narrow to fit inside the long, slim body. A baby snake's lungs are so small they are delicate and prone to infection."

The herpetologist continued, "Your boa has a cold, hopefully not pneumonia. You must use an eyedropper and try very carefully to aspirate (suck out) the mucus and clear the nasal passages. Otherwise, with passages blocked, the snake has no way to breathe when it swallows a mouse; it can't survive without air for as long as it takes a mouse to pass down its throat. Gradually, and slowly, try to suck the mucus out of each nostril. Do this several times a day…Also, your snake needs protein; it has to eat, or it will die. Try to get some blood from fresh meat. Use the eyedropper again, of course washing it thoroughly between usage…."

We didn't often eat red meat. Liquid from raw chicken was watery and diluted. I wasn't able to get much blood at all into the eyedropper. Secret grew weaker and I worried. I picked up my limp baby snake and cradled him in my hand. *How was I going to save my snake?* I decided to try something I am embarrassed to admit. I got the not-so-bright idea that I could give the snake a little of my own blood!

I carried Secret to the bathroom, got the splinter-removing kit out of the medicine cabinet and sat down on the toilet seat lid. With Secret draped over my leg—I cringe at this—I pricked the end of my finger with a needle and squeezed out a drop of blood.

"What are you doing?" my husband demanded. He surprised the dickens out of me!

Through tears: "I'm afraid he'll die. I'm trying to save his life."

"Why don't you mix up some high protein powder?" he inquired.

"Oh, thank you! What a great idea!" I put Secret back in his cage, returned to the kitchen and mixed some protein powder with warm water in a teacup. I carried the cup and eye dropper to Secret's cage, lifted the lid, reached in and held the snake's head between my fingers. With my other hand, I easily inserted the tip of the eyedropper into his mouth. I gave him a few drops of the high protein liquid, replaced the lid to his cage and called it a night.

Secret seemed a little better the next morning. He raised his head slightly when I brought the eyedropper in close. I gave him more of the dissolved high protein powder—about one half teaspoon. As days went on, Secret, by then quite addicted, reared up like a cobra, weaving from side to side, and performed sort of a snake dance, with his mouth open. He stretched for his high protein drink! And drank as much as I dared give him.

I called the herpetologist. He was amazed! He congratulated me but told me, however, I would need to wean the snake back to pinkie mice. He suggested I buy frozen mice at the pet store because Secret still would be too weak to catch and constrict live ones. That would come later. He asked me to check back in a few weeks.

After successfully thawing out pinkie mice (which I hid in our freezer), I dangled them over Secret's head and he was able to get them down his throat. I thought he was ready to graduate to live mice.

"Not so fast," advised the herpetologist. "You'll have to kill the first few fresh mice." It seemed going from frozen to fresh mice would require a transition period: "For about a month," I was told.

How do I kill baby mice? Could I do that? I wondered. It sounded gruesome. The herpetologist assured me, "It's easy. Don't even take the mouse out of the pet store bag. Just hurl the paper bag at your garage door. One hard thud and the mouse can be fed to your snake. Hold it by the tail, sway it back and forth a bit, and your snake will take it."

Ugh. I tried. But killing a mouse was *not* easy. I guess I didn't throw the bag hard enough. The mouse was merely stunned. This was awful! I was torturing a baby mouse! Me, an animal lover! I pulled the bewildered-looking, cross-eyed mouse out of the bag by its tail. I slung it around like a mini-lasso and heaved it, my eyes closed, straight at the garage door. "BONK." That did it. I picked up the dead mouse by the tail and took it in the house. Secret ate it. No problem.

The process remained a problem for *me,* however. I had to repeat that murderous act several more times before Secret was strong enough to catch and constrict live mice on his own. And by that time, I'd horrified my two young sons. They couldn't believe their sweet mother was slinging mice around by the tail and slamming them against the garage door. They weren't bothered enough, though, to go inside or to turn their heads away. They appeared fascinated to watch my dastardly deeds.

Thankfully, Secret grew strong and healthy and was able to go to school, and I regained my reputation for being a kind person. Secret continued to grow. So big, in fact, he graduated to eating small chickens. But I

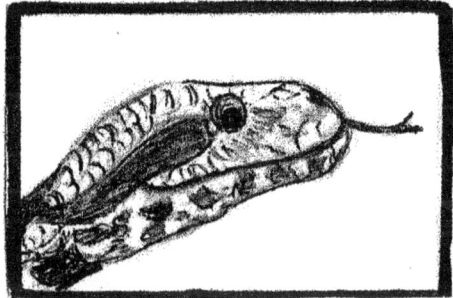

didn't watch. Every few weeks I'd just leave a chicken in his cage (which was now a huge terrarium donated by one of my student's parents). I'd go home, return, and never find the chicken. It was always gone by morning—just a feather here and there.

Secret got as big around as my thigh and over 6 feet long, making some parents a bit anxious. He probably weighed about 25 pounds.

"Isn't he big enough to eat a kid?" I remember one parent nervously asking.

"I don't think so, but I never allow him to get hungry. He's not interested in anything other than chickens. He's very gentle with the children," I offered as comfort.

Secret never even squeezed any of us. Sometimes he would wrap his tail around an arm firmly, just for stability. Snakes are afraid of falling. But Secret was so big, I held the bulk of him, his thick middle, in my lap and supported his head when the children sat around me to touch him. Touching a snake is a real treat—not scratchy or scaly, unless you stroke them backwards. Snakes act a little uneasy with hands near their heads—their tongues dart in and out (to sense smells). Their eyes shift from one object to the next and they draw back, as if in retreat. But if a snake is stroked gently from behind its head toward its tail, it will lie still and calm, perhaps only rippling its strong muscles beneath a person's hand. To the touch, a snake is cool, smooth, and silky.

Nevertheless, it did become clear that a giant boa constrictor was not a good pre-school pet. Before our family moved away, before I left my job at the school, I took Secret back to the pet store. They were thrilled to have a big, now $600+ boa constrictor to sell! They offered credit, not cash, and I learned from the director who replaced me that the pre-school was able to get all pet store supplies free for years and years, plus a rabbit.

3

Queenie, the King Snake

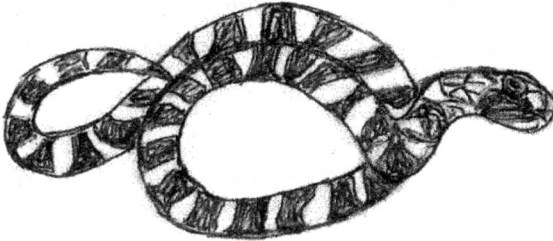

After moving to Orange County and selling the big, beautiful boa constrictor at my last preschool, I needed a snake for my new school setting in Costa Mesa, California. As Director of Hilltop Preschool, I was setting up a "science room" where a science teacher would be present each day for activities or just plain supervising safe handling of animals and equipment.

Jeff (my son) had a friend, Darren Rowe, who was known for finding snakes on Edwards Hill, a (then) deserted, grassy mound of many acres overlooking Huntington Beach. I "hired" Darren, who was about nine years old, to find a non-venomous snake for me. I promised to pay him ten dollars.

Darren found a beauty: a sleek California King snake with glossy rich brown and pale yellow bands. She was a female, with a slim, evenly tapered tail (unlike a male's thicker tail) so we couldn't call her "King." She became "Queenie."

Queenie was mild-mannered from the start. Most King snakes are. They are known to be docile, even though they are very strong for their size, constricting their prey twice as hard as other snakes might. They are called King snakes because they are immune to the poison of all other snakes; even rattlesnake bites do not harm them.

Queenie liked the warmth that comes from being handled by humans. She nestled quite eagerly against my young students' bodies, cozy-ing up to them. She liked to crawl inside sleeves or between buttons on a shirt to wriggle her way to a child's chest or belly, or underarm. She slowly crept her way to children's necks, tickling them around the collar. She "wormed" her way (pardon the expression) to the warmest spots. My students begged for turns to hold Queenie. They even offered to "read" to her, which was fine with me!

Queenie went home with preschoolers' families for many weekends and for all vacations. There was a foster care waiting list for Queenie. She lived happily at the school for at least 10 years! I never knew how old she was since she was fully grown when Darren Rowe found her. She could have been ten years old then. King snakes can live 20—30 years in captivity, so she might have come close to that.

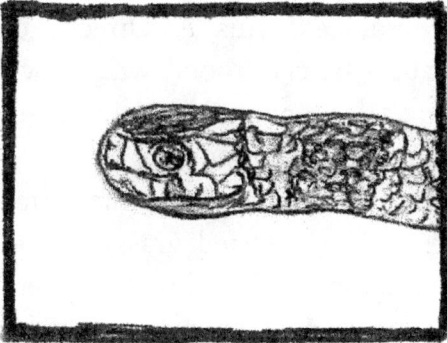

As Queenie got older I worried about needing to replace her someday. Jeff's and Todd's junior high science teacher had a male King snake he was eager to breed so he asked if he could borrow Queenie in hopes of having a slew of baby King snakes—they can lay from 2 to 24 eggs at one time! I agreed to the arrangement. I took Queenie to the K–8 Mesa View School and watched the two King snakes become entangled for hours. Actually, I think they stayed wrapped around each other for days!

Queenie did lay 8 eggs, about 2 weeks later. They looked like off-white, slightly elongated chicken eggs, except with leathery shells, not hard, brittle shells. I carefully followed the science teacher's instructions. With sterile hands, I gently laid the eggs on top of a bed of vermiculite[6] in a plastic shoebox and then covered them with a light layer of more vermiculite, leaving just a bit of the eggs still visible.

I was to keep a light on near the box, carefully monitoring the temperature (to about 75–80 degrees) and once a day I was required to lightly spray or mist the vermiculite—not too much because the development of mold on the eggs was the greatest danger.

Sadly, every one of the eggs exhibited signs of mold—little grey and black dots began to appear on the shells. None of the eggs, or baby snakes, matured—none were viable.

Queenie lived several years beyond that mating experience, but I never tried mating her and hatching eggs again—it was too exacting, too tricky trying to get the temperature, moisture, and exposure to air just right...and so disappointing.

I was discouraged. I felt like a failed midwife. And Queenie seemed depleted after laying eggs. It took her a while to recover her strength.

My funniest memory of Queenie is the number of visitors she had over the years. My graduated students came back to see her frequently. They came to every pre-school open house or after-school family event. Many continued to visit well into their teens! I was touched.

"How nice of you to come see me!" I would genuinely, happily exclaim. I was always delighted to see my former students.

Invariably, after we exchanged hugs and warm greetings, my

6 Vermiculite is a mineral, kind of like soft mica, a soil amendment that is also used for worm farming. It's a common gardening supply. Vermiculite was supposed to mimic the dirt where Queenie would have shallowly buried her eggs in the wild but it was more sterile, to prevent bacteria from invading her eggs.

visiting students would ask, "Where's Queenie? Or, "Is Queenie still here?"

It didn't take long for me to realize my graduates came back for visits faithfully not because of me, but to see Queenie!

Was it because she asked so little of them? *Just hold me and love me.* Or did my students truly learn and come to appreciate the value of being close to, and gently caring for, another living being?

4

Feeding Our Classroom Snake

"Isn't it terribly disturbing for a child to watch a snake eat a live mouse?" one of my student's parents asked long ago.

"At first I thought it might be," I explained. Some children expressed worry about the cute little mouse. But after a while my students learned that those "cute," little mice are really not so adorable—they can be quite stinky. And often mice, even cute little domesticated ones, will bite someone who tries to hold them.

To the contrary, snakes grow on you. They are quiet and fascinating to watch as they move and glide effortlessly without legs. They do not have any odor (unless they are fish-eating snakes, such as garter snakes, for instance[7]). My classroom snakes were tame and NEVER attempted to bite a student. Snakes like to be held; cold-blooded creatures like the comfort and warmth of human bodies.

As my students became more used to seeing snakes and gradually overcame any cultural prejudices of "evil serpents" or fears of the unfamiliar, they developed care for, and attachment to,

---

7   Fish-eating snakes can give off an unpleasant, fishy odor when they are handled.

our classroom snake. They understood the need for snakes to eat. Students certainly didn't want our snake to starve.

My students weren't forced to or required to watch a snake eat a mouse. I always fed the snake at recess time. Students were free to leave the class and go out to recess. Only those who wanted to watch the snake eat were invited to remain in class for the feeding.

It wasn't very far into each year before everyone looked forward to the time to feed our snake (about once a month). Children from other classes, or my former students, heard about this momentous monthly event and begged to come in our class at recess to watch the snake at mealtime.

It always amazed me (1), that kids would be willing to give up recess time for anything! And (2), that kids would be willing to follow my very difficult and stringent expectations for behavior during a feeding.

I asked that students sit on the floor in a circle around the snake's terrarium. If they found themselves crowded, they were welcome to form a second row, an outer circle, and could sit on their knees for a better view. I emptied the snake's cage of its water dish and small hollow log/sleeping den so there was nothing to obscure the snake's or the children's view. I insisted that "NO ONE MOVE" once I dropped a mouse into the snake's enclosure.

Students were permitted to talk quietly and to ask questions. I explained that loud sounds cause vibrations that might distract or frighten the snake. Sudden movements would attract the snake's attention and could cause her to miss the mouse. Movement in the audience could make the snake nervous and not able to concentrate on eating. Sometimes being upset can even cause a snake to throw up. No one wanted to see that occur.

So, there they were, even squirrely little second graders, willing and eager to give up recess, all poised, motionless, waiting attentively in anticipation of the snake eating a live mouse right before their eyes.

I told the students about each step of the process so they would know what to expect and not be alarmed or worried. I made sure each one was seated comfortably before I brought the mouse into the circle. Students *absolutely* should not move once the mouse was put in the snake's cage. Anyone who twitched or had to scratch an itch immediately demonstrated why sitting statue-like was essential. The snake was instantly alerted to the slightest move in the audience as well as to a warm, quivery mouse in the corner or one darting wildly around the terrarium.[8] It was blatantly clear that a child's slightest movement got the snake's attention. She would snap her head around to glare at the student who dared to move.

You see, when a snake is preparing to swallow a mouse, it is necessary to perform the most amazing feat; the snake must unhinge or unhook its top jaw from the bottom so that it can stretch the skin on the side of its face wide enough to allow a mouse to pass down its throat. (I asked the students beforehand to put their fingers on the sides of their own jaws, just below their ears and open and close their mouths. They could easily feel that strong joint that has to be unhinged for the snake to swallow something large.)

"Can you imagine," I'd ask my students, "trying to swallow a big whole, un-cut baked potato—fitting it in your mouth and pushing it down your throat? While you're in that process, you have to concentrate, making sure you can still breathe and won't choke. If something distracted you, you'd be in a pretty helpless position, with a potato stuck in your throat. You wouldn't be able to defend yourself if someone grabbed for you; you wouldn't be able to do much of anything! It would be scary. That's how the snake feels. She wants to make sure her surroundings are safe."

---

8 If a mouse ran around like crazy it made the snake's head spin, and it was really hard for the kids not to jump or screech with excitement. But "SHHH," they had to hold still!

"So DON'T MOVE!" I repeated softly, but firmly.

With everyone holding still, the snake watched the mouse in its cage, sometimes for what seemed like forever. Then, BAM! The snake would strike! I warned students about this impending attack. "It will happen fast. Try not to scream or jump. Just suck in your breath and hold it for a few seconds."

The snake almost never missed, usually biting the mouse in the middle of its furry body. If the snake got the mouse by the tail, the mouse might turn around and bite the snake. That would be bad. The snake would need to let go and try again and, hopefully, wouldn't have sustained a serious, very deep bite. If the snake was lucky to bite the mouse's head, the mouse died quickly and was more easily swallowed; it didn't have to be maneuvered around to a headfirst position, which is best. But this kind of direct hit didn't happen very often.

Biting and holding on to the mouse, the snake quickly winds its body around the mouse's body, squeezing the mouse as hard as it can. Even snakes that are not known to be "constrictors" have to squeeze their prey to death. Only venomous snakes don't have to do this. They can kill their prey by injecting venom through their fangs. Of course, my classroom snakes were not poisonous and none had fangs—only tiny teeth along their jaw lines that worked like small barbs or snags, to keep the food from backing away or sliding out.

The snake squeezes the mouse for several minutes, until the mouse stops breathing. Then the snake gradually begins to uncoil and loosen its grip on the mouse. "This is a very important time to hold still," I reminded my students. The snake will look around to make sure it's safe for her to unhook her jaws to swallow the mouse.

Sure enough, the snake seemed to peer at every student, giving them the "once-over." If no one moves, the snake positions herself to put the mouse's head in her mouth. With muscles slowly going in and out, like you might squeeze a tennis ball, trying to draw the ball deeper into your hand, the snake draws the mouse in. The mouse head makes the side of the snake's face bulge; the snake has to unhook its jaws to begin bringing the mouse body in. The snake twists its head from side to side, up and down, and then you can see the skin on the side of its face really stretch. Slowly, the mouse is drawn into and down the snake's throat until only the tail is hanging out of the snake's mouth like a long strand of spaghetti.

It's hard for students not to laugh. Quiet laughter is OK. The snake re-hooks her jaws and doesn't appear to be using so much effort anymore. But you can see the lump of the mouse getting worked down the snake's body.

Everyone is now free to SLOWLY get up and back away, going to the drinking fountain or outside for a few remaining minutes of recess before the bell rings. "Cool," my students say. The best comment came from a little girl: "It's not so bad. The mouse just got hugged to death."

5

Grandpa Jack Goes Airborne

Or, The Only Time I Ever Heard
Grandpa Jack Scream

One Spring, Grandpa Jack and I explored the San Pedro River area near Tucson, Arizona.[9] I've always been interested in early man and the San Pedro River area was named by Smithsonian Magazine as "one of five great places to see evidence of first Americans." So Grandpa and I visited the spot where the Clovis point was found—a stone spear point used to kill bison and mammoths in prehistoric times.

We were particularly eager to bird watch, especially all the hummingbirds. The San Pedro River is the most important riparian area in the entire United States. More than half the species of birds in this country have been seen there! Not all at once, of course, but at different times of the year. And there are miles and miles of hiking trails all along the river, a great opportunity to observe all kinds of wildlife in addition to birds.

Grandpa Jack has an excellent eye for spotting animals. He's a quiet man who doesn't talk a lot but seems to see everything. He does have a deep, commanding voice when necessary, like alerting someone to danger if we're on a challenging hike or rock climbing. He can certainly get a person's attention in order to avoid harm. And Grandpa Jack has a very loud, piercing whistle he uses to let me know where he is when I get lost in the forest while mushroom hunting. (That happens more than I'd like. I lose

---

9   It's now called the San Pedro National Conservation Area of Arizona; 40 miles set aside to preserve an ideal riparian environment.

track of direction when I'm wandering around a thicket of trees concentrating on bumps in the ground.)

There was no chance of getting lost in a wide, meandering, dry, rock-strewn riverbed but still, I was keeping an eye on Grandpa Jack that day we hiked around the San Pedro area. I didn't want to trail too far behind him. I tend to stop to examine every bug and I can't resist picking up unusual looking stones, some of which earn their way into my pockets.

To check on Grandpa Jack's whereabouts, I happened to look up just in time to witness the most surprising, most astounding sight: Grandpa was actually airborne!! No kidding.

My mouth fell open and I sucked in a huge breath; you could have heard it. I swear Grandpa's feet cleared the ground by two or three feet! Not exactly the Olympic high jump, but he hadn't taken a running start. He just went straight up from ground zero!

At the same time Grandpa Jack shot up above the riverbed, he gave out a scream the likes of which I'd never heard! It was a horrific blood-curdling haunted house-type scream.

"AYYYY-YEEE-YAAAH"—really high-pitched, and ear splitting! Even more alarming coming from usually quiet Grandpa.

Oh, my gosh! I scrambled over the bumpy terrain as quickly as I could, so grateful for my walking sticks that kept me from stumbling over all the loose rocks. "What? What is it?" I wanted to know. What had caused such a flying, leaping, shocking scream from Grandpa Jack?

Stuttering, truly stuttering, he managed to mutter, "a-a-a- sss-snake—a big one!"

"Was it a rattlesnake?" I asked.

"How should I know? It was fast. And so was I."

"I'll say."

Curious me, I slowly approached the grasses at the side of the riverbed, hoping for a glance. I didn't see its head—a triangle shaped head could mean it was a rattlesnake. The snake was slithering away quickly. But the tail had no rattles and I was sure the grey, beige, dark brown markings were those of a bull snake (a large gopher snake).[10] That information didn't pacify Grandpa Jack. "I wasn't going to take the time to find out," he grumbled.

---

10 A bull snake is one of the largest snakes in our country. It can grow to be eight feet long! And its markings are similar to a rattlesnake. But it's not venomous.

6

How To Catch A Lizard

It might have been with my 5th grade Girl Scout buddies, or maybe with my brothers on our chicken ranch, that I learned how to catch lizards. We caught lizards for fun. Looking back, I realize this was not a good idea. Lizard catching is not something I'd advise nowadays. Lizards should be caught only for observation and scientific purposes. They eat so many insects and are beneficial if left in the wild. Catching them can be hurtful, to you and to the lizard.

If you really want to catch a lizard, for observation or science, you have to move slowly and carefully at first and then be ready to move incredibly fast when the time is right. It requires a certain level of risk-taking, as well. You have to brace yourself; and prepare yourself to be bitten.

Fence lizards (or Blue Bellies) don't always bite and, if they do, their bite is not too bad. Their bite can leave a "V-shaped" line of little red dots, tiny bits of blood that seep out from the shallow pinpricks made by their very small teeth. It doesn't hurt much but it always made me mad. "Stop that!" And I'd give the lizard's head a flick with a finger from my free hand to make it let go.

Alligator lizards **always** bite. And the bite from an alligator lizard does hurt! Their long, pointed jaws, like a miniature alligator's, are strong. Their teeth are bigger than a fence lizard's teeth and alligator lizards don't let go. Sort of like a Gila monster, alligator lizards hang on. They keep their hold on your finger and seem to try to grind their small teeth in even deeper. Still, their bite is not very deep, but it hurts enough to make you yell.

I was never able to tame an alligator lizard. They stay mean and will always try to bite you. Fence lizards, on the other hand, can be tamed to eat bits of meat or mealworms held in your fingers. You can hold fence lizards in your hand and let them crawl up your arm once they get used to you.

Catching a lizard is tricky. If you see one climbing up a tree, it will run to the other side of the tree the minute it sees you (just as squirrels do).

That's when you have to move fast. Quickly reach around and slap your hand as fast as you can against the other side of the tree. If you guessed correctly, you will have pinned the lizard right smack against the tree. Wrap your fingers around its body; grasp the lizard in your fist, firmly but not so much as to crush it. If you got it in the middle of its body, and not back by its tail, it can't reach its head around to bite your fingers or your thumb. Good deal.

If you manage to grab a lizard by just the tail, it can (and usually will) turn around and bite. It also may pull away, leaving its tail behind—and a tail is all that you will have in your hand. To escape, most lizards can let go of their tails. They drop their tails for defense. When a lizard detaches its tail, it confuses its predators. A bird, for instance, will focus on the still-wiggling tail, giving the lizard time to get away. Most lizards can regenerate or grow their tails back in a few months. But you really don't want it running around without proper defense.

It's too bad I didn't learn a much easier and safer, less hurtful, way to catch a lizard until I was 69 years old. As an old grandma, I took a class from Dr. Michael Parker at the Siskiyou Field Institute in Selma, Oregon. It was a class titled "Reptiles and

Amphibians." We learned a lot, catching numerous specimens out in the field, and then letting them go, of course. We never injured one. One of the most valuable lessons for me was learning to make a "lizard lasso." Here is what is written, word for word, in my field notes.

Observations: We made lizard lassos. We tied dental floss ("waxed, mint floss works best") to the end of a 6-foot long narrow piece of bamboo, making a one to two inch noose out of the dental floss. The floss noose can actually be dangled in front of a lizard's snout without disturbing the lizard. Carefully positioning the noose over the lizard's head and then giving a quick, but gentle tug, we were all able to capture lizards! Easy-peasy.

7

Sally, the Salamander

There is beautiful camping all along the California coast. One of our favorite family spots was Refugio State Campground. It had beach access for water and sand play, of course, but it also had a creek at the other end of camp that beckoned little boys to explore.

Fast-moving rivulets among the smooth rocks were ideal for leaf-boat races. Quiet pools of water displayed all sorts of small snails scuttling along the bottom and an abundance of boatmen and water striders "walking" in jerky motions all across the surface of ponds, every which way.[11] Butterflies floated in the air; iridescent dragonflies flitted and darted, aiming for the water, then zipping to the sky. The creek was like a fairy tale—an idyllic riparian environment, lush with ferns and greenery and large thick-branched trees. Best of all, critters could be found by overturning rocks at the water's edge. Imagine lifting off the roof of a busy subway—all sorts of creatures skittering and squirming

---

11 These insects have long, strong, skinny legs with tiny hairs that repel the water so the insect stays dry, on top of the water, and does not get heavy and sink.

this way and that: beetles, centipedes, worms, spiders, sand fleas and—if you hit the jackpot—a salamander!

California salamanders are varied. The ones Todd and Jeff found were mostly California newts. (Newts are salamanders but usually with slightly drier, bumpier skin—not as wet and slippery or as elongated as many salamanders.) Some California salamanders are called fire belly or red-bellied newts because their undersides are a bright, shiny orange or red-orange color.

The backs of the newts we found were more subdued in color, like a redwood tree. The bumps on their back are tiny—pinhead sized little pebbles—not as rough as sandpaper, but more leathery and moist.

Salamanders are beguiling with big, buggy eyes that stare right at you. They look at you curiously, innocently, sort of like they're wondering what comes next. They have cute little, slightly pointed noses and four adorable pinkish or sometimes yellow-tinged toes on baby hands and feet. (Sometimes the back feet have five toes). Salamanders are defenseless; they have no teeth or claws. All they can do is hide to keep safe.

"Please, please, Mom," our boys begged. "Can't we adopt *one*? Just take *one* home? We'd be so careful with it."

"No. Salamanders need to be where it's cool and damp. They eat lots of live insects. Catching that many bugs a day and making sure the insects stayed inside the salamander cage would be a real chore. Salamanders belong in their natural environment. One wouldn't live long at our house," I'd firmly explain.[12]

So Todd and Jeff learned to enjoy playing gently with the salamanders during our camping trips. The newts crawled across their hands and up their arms, hanging on with their rounded toes that looked like they had small suction cups at the ends. They tiptoed along very lightly.

---

12 Actually, I was wrong. Later I learned that salamanders could live 10-15 years in the wild and 20 or more years in captivity!

Who knows how or why the boys caught me at a weak moment one year. I finally gave in to their pleas and permitted them to bring *one* salamander home. They named her Sally.

Reddish-brown, four-inch long Sally ate all the ants the boys caught; she couldn't seem to get her fill. Todd, at age six, was unusually patient as he crouched by her aquarium with a tiny bit of hamburger meat stuck on his protruding wiggly finger. By golly, he actually taught Sally to eat tiny portions of ground meat right from his hand! She grew fat and saucy, marching across the kitchen linoleum on slightly raised legs, preventing her round belly from touching the floor. She didn't care for the carpeting much and seldom worked her way across the rug. It was slower going on the carpet and she paused now and then to shake a leg, as if ridding her foot of some unwanted debris. The boys kept a careful watch over her travels. She could cover a surprising amount of ground if you didn't keep an eye on her.

After a few years, Sally got more adventurous and accustomed to the different walking surfaces. She was faster and, over time, the boys must have gotten more lackadaisical about their supervision of Sally's outings. Tragedy struck! Sally walked across the living room carpet and stepped onto the electric outlet on the floor! ZAP! Damp amphibian little Sally was electrocuted.

In tears, the boys came to me holding out Sally's motionless form. I laid the small body on a paper towel on the kitchen counter and instructed the woeful looking boys to prepare for Sally's funeral and backyard burial. Todd and Jeff found a small box and lined it with grasses and rose petals—very sweet. I picked up

Sally's body to place her in the pretty coffin and then it was my turn to be stunned! Sally's throat was throbbing! The little patch of smooth skin under her head was definitely moving in and out!

We were overjoyed! Sally had evidently just been in "reptile shock,"[13] amphibian that she was. She recovered! For several years after that shocking incident (pardon the pun) Sally marched around the house as usual, but only on three legs. The leg that stepped into the floor socket shriveled up and was useless to her. Todd and Jeff never let her out of their sight and Sally lived a long time, as salamanders are known to do.

---

13 Wild Life Rescue reports that reptiles may go into temporary shock when they have experienced some trauma.

8

Ted and Linoleum

My sons, Todd and Jeff, happily caught grey-green California toads of all sizes, whenever we camped at Lake Cachuma, near Santa Barbara, California. We were careful not to harm critters in the wild and very rarely took any home. Two exceptions were Ted and Linoleum. We didn't harm those toads, but we did take them home, where they survived happily ever after…almost. California western toads typically can live for one to ten years in the wild, but up to forty years in captivity! They make good pets if you don't mind their often-muddy bodies. They can be tamed to eat out of your hand and like to nestle comfortably in a person's palm. Toads **do not** give you warts.

Linoleum was quite a bit smaller than Ted. Ted was fist-sized. Linoleum measured about one third of that—the size of a tangerine, compared to a large orange. In spite of what appeared to be an unfair advantage, Todd and Jeff pitted them against one another in all sorts of competitions—all very amusing.

The toads raced one another across our swimming pool, when the boys plopped them in. The toads took turns at being declared "the winner!" The comic demonstration of the "frog-kick" kept us all laughing for the entirety of the race; sometimes we couldn't stop laughing even after the race ended. Imagine fat, round bodies, propelled in jerky motions by skinny freckled back legs bent at the "knees" pointing out almost at right angles to the left and to the right of the toads' bodies. Their legs were not under them, aimed toward the bottom of the pool, but stuck out at the sides, bending and then straightening toward the back in rhythmic motions like wind-up toys. The bent legs would snap back and propel the toads in a spurt, straight ahead.

"Straight ahead" did vary, however, prompting race attendees on the pool deck to scream and yell and jump up and down, cheering on one toad or another. "No, no! Don't turn left!" Toads don't have ears, so I'm not sure if they could hear their coaches or if they were aware of their fans rooting for them. They do sense vibrations through their mouths and lungs, even their skin; some-how they can "hear" or react to a dog bark, for instance.

Ted and Linoleum had even more peculiar races across the front lawn. Bugs, dandelions or large blades of grass were distractions, leading the toads to crawl and hop in all different directions, occasionally back to the starting line! The toads were well exercised but not overly so. They simply stop when they've had enough. They stop and puff their sides in and out, blinking, otherwise remaining motionless.

Ted and Linoleum, when not performing for neighborhood kids, were well taken care of. They were fed various insects, mostly mealworms, sometimes by hand, 'til their sides bulged (more than usual) and they

burped repeatedly. They lived in a good-sized terrarium, with ample mud for digging, and a generous water dish. Efforts to beautify their enclosure met with failure, however. Attempts to add greenery proved hopeless; they trampled everything into the mud.

Sadly, when our family was on vacation, leaving the toads' care to the teenager next door, Linoleum did not survive. The toad-sitter fed them their mealworms, but neglected to re-fill their water dish. Linoleum got dehydrated and died. Ted dug deep down in the damp mud and was OK. So okay, in fact, he went on to live many years longer.

9

Ted, The Toad With Nearly Nine Lives

Todd sometimes boasted that Ted was "The Toad-with-Nine-Lives." Like cats are said to be able to survive nine close calls or death-defying experiences in a lifetime, it seemed Ted could, too! Digging into the mud and living through that deadly drought that killed his companion, Linoleum, was Ted's first demonstration of his survival skills.

And then there was the broken leg fiasco. "Mom, don't you remember when Ted visited your preschool and one of your kids, playing dress-up, stepped on him with a high-heeled shoe?" I didn't remember. I must have repressed that one.

Todd insisted, "You put a splint on Ted's broken leg, made out of popsicle sticks and masking tape." I still couldn't recall. Todd swears it was true. He assured me that Ted's leg healed with no problem, though Ted was pretty laughable hobbling around with a lopsided gait, like a pirate dragging his peg leg behind him. That was close call Number Two.

The third time Todd thought Ted was a goner was when he was spotted, with eyes popping, peering out of the clenched jaws of Bob, our big, black Labrador retriever. Ted released the toxins from his poison glands (the parotid glands) behind his eyes and, thankfully, Bob dropped him immediately.

Concern for the toad was quickly transferred to worries about our dog, now beginning to foam at the mouth! Fortunately, for some odd reason we knew the remedy was to give Bob milk or ice cream. We gave him both. And both Ted and Bob survived that incident, which was never repeated. Bob learned that Toads are not edible.

Rambo, our cat, already knew that. Rambo was smarter than Bob, the dog. But Rambo also was interested in Ted toad—not as food but for amusement. Somehow Ted made it through yet another potentially deadly encounter. (This was the fourth time his life was spared.) Our cat pounced on Ted! Todd wasn't far away and spotted Rambo batting Ted back and forth between his paws. Todd was able to shoo off Rambo in time, so that Ted escaped with only a minor cut and a few scratches.

Ted's fifth chance to continue living was one of the most serious. He was swimming freely around our backyard pool when Todd noticed him heading toward the side where the filter basket and filter intake system was located. Todd saw the leaf filter basket had been removed and was resting on top of the pool deck. It had not been replaced! That meant that there was nothing to catch leaves—or Ted! Anything circulating by that area could be sucked directly into the filter system, with no basket as a catchall.

Todd sped around to the side, but not in time.

Ted, swimming with all his might, front legs in a frantic, fast-paced "frog-stroke," had been pulled right into the pipes! Todd reached in, grabbed the pipe loose and pulled it out of the water. That section of plastic pipe was about 5 inches long. Ted's head and front legs jutted

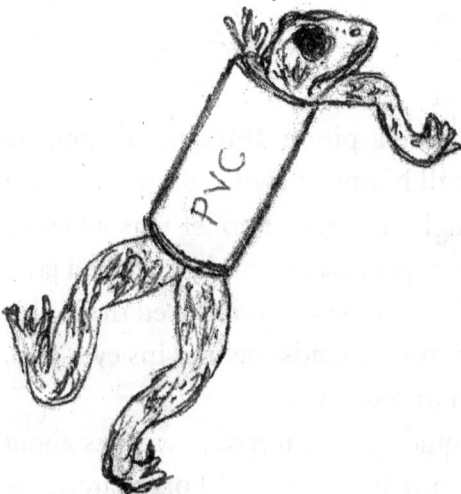

out of one end, and his back legs, squashed together, stuck out the other end of the pipe. His body, squeezed and elongated, was inside! Todd gently prodded and poked from the back and Ted was finally able to pop out the front! He was OK. Ted was OK. Todd *still* gets tense talking about it. Ted came really close to getting sucked into the pool filter! His life nearly ended on the 5th close call.

But, unbelievable as it is, Ted continued to live; he even went on to college!

10

Ted Goes to College

After about eight years of Ted the Toad being an important part of our household, living in his muddy terrarium in Todd's room, it was time for Todd to go off to college, to say goodbye to Ted. He couldn't do it.

Todd asked if pets were permitted in the dorm. "Not allowed," they said, "only fish." Todd reasoned that Ted did live in an old aquarium, like a fish would, but Ted's enclosure was one that wasn't filled with water and so should be preferable for a dorm room—no chance of leaking or spillage. Therefore, both Todd and Ted headed off to USC![14]

Ted was *more* than welcome to stay. His presence was found to be highly desirable on an old campus in the middle of the inner city. The dormitory was infested with cockroaches! Ted flung out his long sticky pink tongue and flicked a 'roach' into his mouth the minute Todd plunked one into his cage.

While he was in his room studying, Todd let Ted roam freely, hopping here and there, searching for cockroaches to his heart's (and bulging stomach's) content.

Visitors began to notice that no bugs were crawling around Todd's dorm room, as they did throughout the rest of the building. It wasn't long before Todd's friends asked if they could "rent" Ted the Toad for an evening. I have no idea if there was an actual charge for his services.

I do know that all went well until Ted was returned one night apparently feeling quite ill. He slowly crept to his water dish, climbed in, and stayed there…not moving. Did he overeat? Toads can be quite gluttonous.

---

14 The University of Southern California, in Los Angeles.

When Ted was still in his water dish the next day, Todd was concerned. After inquiring, he found out that the friend's roommate had earlier sprayed insecticide, RAID, in that room. They concluded that Ted must have ingested a cockroach that had been sprayed, but somehow survived. Ted remained in his water dish for several days; then emerged, crawled around his terrarium, and seemed fine. Evidently he was able to soak out the toxins. It seems that the toad that Todd later claimed, "Had Nearly Nine Lives" was going on to live life number six.

Worse than Ted's near death in a swimming pool filter was his tumble from the third floor balcony of the dormitory on the USC campus. Todd planned to have a big party in his dorm room and worried that Ted's aquarium, even in a corner spot, might get accidentally kicked and broken. Todd placed the aquarium outside on his small balcony, where he was sure Ted would be safe. It proved not to be so.

Somehow, when Todd went out to retrieve Ted the next day, the aquarium was on its side, and no Ted. Ted was not on the balcony. The small drainage hole was far too small for a big toad to have squeezed down. The only escape would have been under the metal railing and over the side, falling to the ground, three stories below!

Todd peered over, dreading what he expected to see. But there was no sign of a flattened toad on the sidewalk around the dorm. Todd raced down to the first floor, out the main door, and to the area directly below his balcony. No Ted. Then, on careful inspection of the bushes alongside the walkway, he spied a barely-alive toad. Carefully, Todd lifted the non-moving Ted and gingerly carried him back upstairs. Once in his water dish, Ted remained motionless. There was still visible throbbing on his throat and he blinked occasionally. Ted remained in his water dish for days and finally reached out one stiff leg, then another. He was able to eat mealworms from Todd's fingers, though his aim was off and he missed more times than not. Ted eventually recovered to go on to "Life Number Seven."

Lucky Life Number Seven turned out to be charmed. Word of Ted's survival spread around campus. Todd's friend, Link, who was an art major, designed a T-shirt—one that had an enlarged black and white photo of Ted on the front, emblazoned with the words, "Ted" above the picture and "Toad of the 80s" below Ted's face. Link made 30 shirts that sold out immediately. Todd never even got one but chuckled out loud every time he saw someone wearing a "Ted, Toad of the 80s," shirt on his or her way to class.

Another friend of Todd's, a biology major, told Todd that her professor was interested and asked if Todd could bring Ted to the science lab one day. He did. He and Ted were greeted by an effusive young woman who declared, "My, aren't you a handsome toad?" She asked if she could do a small scraping of skin from one of Ted's toes, needing some cells to do an age test. It turned out that Ted proved to be 29 years old!! But the professor said she had bad news: "Ted was a female toad."

Ted, Toad of the 80s, turned out to be Teddy or Theodosia or Theodora. Never mind, we all knew that female toads are usually the larger of the species—and Ted had always appeared very well fed, definitely on the large side. In spite of the gender change revelation, we continued to refer to Ted as "he."

For Life Number eight, Ted (and Todd) graduated from USC and went off to graduate school at the University of Houston. Would Ted survive the long, hot car trip across mountains and deserts? Again, he survived. Todd kept Ted's aquarium in the passenger seat all the way, only moving the enclosure when necessary to keep it out of the bright sun.

Ted's ninth life was one of decrepit old age. He moved as though he had arthritis—very slowly and deliberately, and not much. He was nearly blind, often staring a long time at bugs crawling around his terrarium, as if he was not sure he saw something moving. He'd re-position himself, in jerky motions, to get a better angle; still he'd often miss his prey. Todd had to feed Ted by hand, not just now and then, but all the time. Then, it was almost force-feeding, prying open and gently putting a mealworm between Ted's toothless jaws, pushing it into the toad's mouth. Ted continued to deteriorate and, one day, simply stopped living. It was the end of 32 adventurous years.

11

Cricket Story

"Babies! Zillions of little cricket babies!" I happily exclaimed aloud to no one but me in my 2nd grade classroom. The room, however, now devoid of students in the late afternoon hours, was anything but empty and silent. The guinea pig chortled happily in his cage; adult crickets chirped in unison, water bubbled in the fish bowl, even the snake could be heard softly rustling through dry bark in her glass enclosure. My classroom, also alive with lizards and toads, mealworms and silkworms, had the odor of, I liked to think, a clean, welcoming pet store. Colorful children's artwork, and many samples of 2nd grade story writing adorned the walls, bright evidence of much going on.

But I thought, *I can't lock up as usual and leave everything here for the weekend. I have to take my baby crickets home. They'll need tending to. I've got to keep sponge pieces moist for their drinking water. They're so tiny they'll drown in that shallow water dish. And I can't wait to show them to my son, Jeff! He'll be amazed by my zillions of babies!* I corrected myself, *Well, maybe not zillions. But I bet there are dozens and dozens.*

I smiled, proudly admiring my tiny ½ centimeter, ant-sized, perfectly formed miniature crickets actively hopping around, bouncing off the glass sides of their terrarium.

After a slow, careful drive home, without any abrupt stops or starts at traffic lights, cricket babies and I arrived safely. With my purse over my shoulder, I eased out of the car, and closed the door quietly so as not to jar the little ones. Then, quickly, in my excitement, I zipped around to the passenger side, eager to show the cricket babies to Jeff, whom I was sure would be home from high school by now.

Once again, resuming a slower pace, I gently opened the car door. I muttered, "O.K., babies, everything's OK," as I carefully unlatched the seat belt that held their terrarium in place. Little black dots hopped all over the container, going crazy, no matter how deftly I eased my fingers under the bottom edges of their enclosure and smoothly slid it out of the car. With short, mincing steps, I made my way to the front door. Supporting the aquarium, holding it against my body with my left hand, and partially with my right, I was able to free my right thumb and forefinger to make a slight turn of the doorknob.

The door opened easily and there was Jeff (*hurray*) just as I had imagined, stretched out on the sofa, facing me as I entered. "Jeff, wait 'til you see my babies!"

My son raised his eyebrows and gave me that unsmiling, but neutral, ready-for-anything look that said, "What now, Mom?"

"Wait 'til you see my baby crickets! I have hundreds of them!"

In my eagerness to reach Jeff's side, to show off my babies, my toe caught on the edge of the avocado green shag carpet, where it met the tile of the front hall. I gasped. And so did Jeff.

What happened next is a blur.

Looking ahead to catch my footing, I saw Jeff's wide-open eyes suddenly scrunch closed, his brows furrow, and his lips press together—his relaxed features now squeezed tightly, as if to shut out the unfolding disaster.

"Oh, no!" In my stumbling over the rug, the screened top to the dry aquarium flipped off, the enclosure tilted forward at an angle too precarious. Zillions (or was it just dozens?) of baby crickets, and their parents, disappeared instantaneously into the shag carpeting, hopping in as if the thick green fibrous strands were a field of grass. On hands and knees, with fingers cupped, so as not to squash the scratchy, wiggly insects, I was able to retrieve some adult crickets, but the majority made it into the rug, or the unlit fireplace area, while others scooted under the sofa or into the kitchen. So much for my baby crickets; I'd lost them all.

I could tell that Jeff really wanted to laugh. He put his hands to his mouth to stifle what I thought sounded like fake coughs or muffled chuckles. Actually, I suspect it was a combination of feelings: of amusement (at another of his mother's goofs) and feelings of horror at the thought of all those bugs loose in the house. "Sorry about your cricket babies, Mom. That's too bad."

Amazingly, it didn't turn out to be so bad after all. I was able to raise more cricket babies with the adults I'd picked up from the carpeting. And cheerful cricket chirpings were now heard at home as well as in my classroom. "Crickets bring good luck," I'd tell my own children and my students. "The Chinese keep them in little cages, as household pets and reminders of good fortune."

Sometimes it was a bit embarrassing for both my sons, Todd and Jeff, when they had friends over to visit. Cricket chirps were often heard in the house, loud and clear—too distinct to be outside sounds. Jeff would tell guests, "Don't worry. Those are my Mom's fireplace crickets talking to the kitchen crickets."

For years and years, the descendants of those dropped baby crickets had nightly conversations from room to room. We moved away from that Huntington Beach house but, for all I know, the crickets may still be there, talking to one another.

12

Once I Held A Tarantula

It was at a Ranger-held campground program where I had the opportunity to hold a tarantula. Not that I was eager. I was quite afraid, in fact. But I thought that my sons should know about creatures in the wild, so I took them to the educational Ranger programs every chance I could.

The Ranger spoke very calmly as a giant hairy tarantula crawled all over his hands and arms. He insisted that tarantulas are quite docile and will only bite if they are cornered or provoked.[15] And, he went on, "their bites may be painful but not terribly poisonous—sort of like a bee or a wasp sting." *No, thank you. I'm not into pain*, I thought to myself, *nor do I want my boys to be bitten in case they should happen to aggravate that critter.*

The Ranger invited everyone in the audience to form a circle. Each person was instructed to hold out a hand, palm up, so the tarantula could travel from one person's hand to the next. My boys were willing to try it so I hid my apprehensions and joined them up front. The Ranger was careful to keep his hands beneath ours, ready to catch a dropped spider, should that be necessary. It

---

15 Later I did some research. What the Ranger said was true: "New World" tarantulas (from the New World—the Americas) are evidently not as aggressive as "Old World" tarantulas—those from Asia, Africa, Australia, and Europe.

wasn't. He kept talking: "Don't worry. If the tarantula is upset it will rear up on its hind legs, and show its fangs. It will give you plenty of warning if it is about to bite. There will be no surprises. Nothing to fear."

When my turn came, I was afraid, of course. *Would the spider know?* (Dogs, and other animals seem to know when people are afraid.)

Evidently not. The spider marched deliberately across my hand, right on to the next person's. All I felt was dainty, barely perceptible small touches of its feet. Whew! Was I proud to meet that challenge and come away smiling!

My exciting, positive experience holding a tarantula in the campgrounds gave me the bright idea of getting a pet tarantula for my classroom. It turned out to be a good idea, for a while. The world's biggest spider is fascinating to watch. It ate mealworms and crickets (which I raised in my class) so it was easy to feed. However, I never could muster up the courage to take the spider out of its terrarium. *What if it should rear up and threaten one of my students?* I just wasn't willing to take the chance.

Then a parent asked me, "Don't you worry when you clean the cage that one of the tarantula's hairs could get in your eye? Those hairs can cause terrible eye infections, even blindness." Yikes! No one told me that! So I inquired right away.

I found out there *is* a possibility of flying tarantula hairs— when I clean the cage or when the spider cleans or grooms itself. One reason New World Tarantulas don't often bite is because they can protect themselves by scratching the hairs on their bellies and shooting them at predators. The hairs on a tarantula aren't really hairs—they are bristles (called setae), sometimes barbed— that can stick to skin and cause irritation, and they *can* create terrible problems if they get into someone's eye.

So much for keeping a pet tarantula—I returned it to the pet store.

13

Stinkbugs

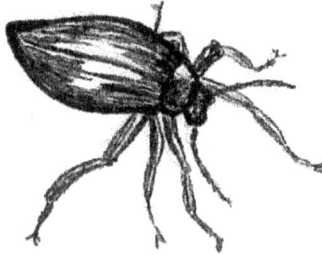

Grandpa Jack grew up on a chicken farm in north Texas, and then became a mountaineer. Both experiences contributed to his knowledge about and respect for most animals. The only animals he hated were marmots. [16] Grandpa Jack did not care for stinkbugs or skunks either.

I agreed with his assessment of skunks. I don't care for their odor at all. I will admit stinkbugs do stink, but their scent is not *that* bad, perhaps a little bitter or acrid to the nose. Grandpa Jack says it *is* bad. I guess if you step on one, as he did sometimes in Texas, then it might be a pretty strong smell. But even hiking in the desert, I was always careful never to squash one. Opposite to Grandpa, I was crazy about stinkbugs! I was always on the lookout for them. I'd even pick them up. They don't bite and they don't skitter around like most critters. They walk very slowly and carefully and just tickle a little crossing your hand or traveling up your arm. But I wouldn't want a stinkbug walking across my face!

---

16 Marmots are cute, furry little rodents, like fat squirrels, that live in the mountains and are very good at getting into backpackers' packs. They steal things, especially food, quietly and quickly. Grandpa used to say he was going to write a book: "100 Ways to Cook Marmot." He never did. As far as I know, people don't eat marmots.

Ugh. (Come to think of it, I don't like dogs licking my face either.)

I came to appreciate stinkbugs so much because they were excellent teaching tools for my classroom. I thought it was important to teach kids about animal classification—learning about all the different families of animals. If you learn to identify different animals, you can look at various things, even ideas, and know how to sort them out, figure out what they might be.

Classifying animals and organizing all sorts of information may sound a bit boring but I guarantee stinkbugs are *not* boring! My students were intrigued with them; they appreciated them as much as I did. Stinkbugs are pretty big—an inch or two long. They are very black and shiny and their features are perfectly clear. It's easy to see their six legs and their three body parts; that makes them an insect and not a spider. Because of their size, they can look scary at first, but they're not.

Stinkbugs are slow, quiet, easy-going, easy to pick up, and they don't hurt at all. They're funny to watch, creeping around, examining their surroundings. And some of the boys in my classroom also thought they were funny to tease. It was a big joke to give the stinkbug a small jab on their way to the pencil sharpener. Stinkbugs raise their little bums, like a skunk raises its tail, to give a warning. Enough poking and teasing caused a stinkbug to stink. That's its protection. "Yeewww," everybody in class would moan, when one of the stinkbugs was irritated enough to give off an odor. I didn't find it as funny as the kids did; I worried about my stinkbug's safety. (Thankfully, I never lost one.)

You can tell, I really cared about my beautiful bugs. And I knew, for sure, that Grandpa Jack really cared about me when he gave me one. We were camping at Joshua Tree, in the California desert, just packing up to return home. Evidently, a stinkbug was enjoying the shade under our tent. Grandpa Jack spotted the bug when he rolled up the ground cloth. He scooped up the bug and handed it to me in a plastic sandwich bag. "Here. I knew you'd like this," he said, turning his head to the side, with a look of disgust on his face. He held the bag far out in front of him; not wanting to be one bit close to a critter he disliked and feared would stink up a storm. I was so pleased. Happy to have a beautiful new specimen for my classroom and touched that Grandpa Jack would put his own feelings aside to give me something he knew I'd appreciate…even if he didn't. But he didn't suspect I'd want to take it home. He thought he was just handing it to me for observation and admiration. Then we'd let it go.

"I can't let it go," I wailed. "I need it in my class."

"And how do you think you're going to get it home? I can't allow a stinkbug in the truck. It could stink up the truck forever. We'd never be able to get the smell out!"

I figured out a way. Putting the bug in and hanging Grandpa's water bottle outside the truck was out of the question. I knew that the minute I saw his horrified expression at my suggestion.

"Absolutely not!" Grandpa Jack declared with a deep frown and a grimace. So I put the stinkbug in an empty plastic milk jug, punched holes in the jug for air, and tied that newly made bug cage securely to the outside of the truck. Grandpa begrudgingly agreed I could do that. The stinkbug made it home and lived happily ever after. The end.

14

The Baby Octopus

My boyfriend, Ronnie Cooper, and I had a baby octopus as a pet for a while. Ronnie was my boyfriend in 6th grade. He was six inches shorter than I, but so cute. We went to different schools for junior high and didn't see one another for years. Then we met up again in high school, when we were 16 and 17. By that time, I was the one who was six inches shorter! Ronnie wasn't what the girls called "cute" anymore; he was head turning, movie-star gorgeous! And he was my best friend. My dad had died the previous year and Ronnie said it was like I was wandering in a dark tunnel. He described himself as "the light at the end of the tunnel;" but he said when I emerged back into the sunshine, I wouldn't need him anymore. We did go our separate ways after I went off to college.

However, that senior year in high school we were inseparable, spending every waking moment together. (Even a few sleeping moments when his family took me to Catalina Island with them for a water-skiing week vacation. That's another story.) On weekends, we started out really early, hiking in the Malibu Mountains so Ronnie could fish at the lake. I read or collected wildflowers while he fished. Sometimes we drove across the mountains to spend the day at Malibu Beach. That's when we found our baby octopus.

Besides swimming and sunning and making elaborate sand castles, we enjoyed beachcombing and especially picking through the piles of kelp that washed up onto the sand. Those piles held all sorts of treasures: unbroken, rare shells, sea stars, and urchins. We never knew what all we'd find.

"Huh!" Ronnie audibly sucked in his breath and quickly withdrew his hand from the slimy seaweed. A little octopus had grabbed him and clung to his wrist and forearm. Its body was the size of a golf ball, but the tentacles, all eight, were at least 6 inches long. Its round body pulsed in and out; it looked at Ronnie beseechingly with round, bulgy black eyes. "Hurry, go get our sand bucket. Fill it with seawater. Quick!" Ronnie commanded. I followed orders. Very carefully, as Ronnie submerged the little critter into the bucket, he gradually helped the octopus release its sticky tentacles from his hand and arm. It still seemed to keep its eyes on Ronnie.

Was I surprised when Ronnie announced, "We're taking him home. We'll set up a salt water aquarium and take care of this baby." We filled up every container we could find with water from the ocean and drove home slowly and carefully. Ronnie repeatedly asked me, "How's he doing?" The little guy (or was it a girl?) was doing just fine, but still looking worried, I thought.

As soon as we got home, Ronnie rushed around to set up an aquarium he had in the garage. He put it on the desk right next to his bed. He installed an air pump and some sort of filter. "The octopus will need oxygen circulating in the water," Ronnie explained.

We looked up all we could about maintaining salt-water aquariums and keeping an octopus in captivity. That was in the "olden days," the 1950s, before computers and smart phones of the 2000s. There was no notion of "Googling" anything, down-loading apps, or listening to any iPods. We thought we were fortunate to have an encyclopedia set available (Encyclopedia

Britannica, no less). We checked out books from the library and talked to pet store and aquarium owners.

We learned that a salt-water aquarium is much more complicated to maintain than fresh water ones. Keeping the temperature cool enough was a big issue. And keeping the tank clean was another. We would have to go to the ocean often to get fresh salt-water! The octopus needed live food. I think we fed it guppies; I don't remember for sure. We found out that octopi don't live very long in captivity—maybe a few years at most. But Ronnie was determined to keep this baby and take good care of it.

We observed and then found out we were right: octopi are intelligent and they can demonstrate affection for their human owners. Our baby rushed out of its flowerpot-hiding place every time Ronnie entered the room. It seemed to hide from other people. When Ronnie or I put our hands into the aquarium it came to us and stuck around (ha-ha) to be gently stroked. It, literally, attached itself to us by its tentacles with the many suction cups; and we became quite attached to our baby octopus.

We rushed home from school every day, and darted in the door to check on our pet. It zoomed out of its corner hiding to greet us. One day, I remember, we were particularly anxious to get home to see how it was doing. The temperature that day was unusually warm.

It was hot—too hot. And how very sad it turned out to be. Our octopus was floating limply toward the top of the tank. Not dead, but noticeably weak, clinging to us with very little strength. It died soon after that.

"Ron" was a tall, muscular, macho, football player, and an I'm-in-control kind of guy. What most people didn't know was that Ronnie was also kind, gentle, thoughtful and sensitive. He sat down on the edge of his bed, elbows on knees, his handsome face hidden behind his hands, and he cried.

15

Gus, the Guinea Pig

Gus was the cutest critter of them all. He was a cinnamon and white, mostly smooth-haired, common guinea pig. He did have some funny tufts of hair here and there; sort of like crazy cowlicks that gave him a "bad hair day" look every day. Bits of fur that stuck up or twisted awry added to his dopey, sleepy, "just-got-up," confused-looking, not-very-smart expression. Gus was never confused about someone approaching his cage, however. He was always hopeful; always sure anyone who came near had to be a friend. He wiggled and squirmed and squealed with delight: "Squeak, squeak, squeak."

Gus lived happily in my first and second grade classrooms, far beyond the four or five years typical of a guinea pig's life expectancy. Every morning, as soon as I put my key in the door, I could hear Gus shrieking with glee: "squeak, squeak, squeak." He kept up his high-pitched chattering until I reached in and petted him. Then he'd purr and chortle with contentment and finally quieted down after he had fresh water and his food dish was filled anew.

The squeaking and squealing started again as my students entered the room. He greeted each one and they greeted him in return: "Hi, You"…"Hey, Gus, how are you today?" "It's OK, Gus, we're here now…" Somehow, once class began, Gus knew to be quiet. There would be occasional squeaky outbursts if a child walked close to Gus' cage on his or her way to the pencil sharpener or drinking fountain, or if a student finished work early and went over to read to Gus.

My students were always free to read (or to write) once an assignment was completed. Getting to read to Gus was a great incentive to finish work. After a few squeaks, Gus snuggled into a student's lap and appeared to be quite attentive—he'd peer at the pages of a book, only sometimes attempting to nibble on a page as it was turned. My students adored him. Gus was held and petted daily. What a charmed life!

On weekends and vacation times, Gus was "adopted" by, and went home with, students. There was always a waiting list of adoptive families. I remember one particularly funny incident. The child involved didn't think it was funny; it was traumatic for her. Vanessa's mother was from Ecuador. When she, her brother, younger sister, and her Mom brought Gus home for the weekend, their father, returning from work, grinned and exclaimed, "Oh, great! A cavy for dinner!" (Cavy is the name for wild guinea pigs found in South America.)

"No, Dad, no! That's Gus. He's not for eating!" Vanessa's father was teasing, of course, even though cavies really are considered good food in South American countries, sort of like rabbit meat. Vanessa never took Gus home for the weekend again; she worried that her father might have been serious about wanting to have Gus for dinner. She didn't want to take a chance.

At about six or seven years old, Gus began showing his age. Squeaks weren't as loud and piercing; his full, round body became more slight and fragile—you could actually feel his little bones when you picked him up. Gus still purred and chortled and let the students know he appreciated their loving, gentle attention.

He still liked to be held and to have students read to him.

One morning, when I arrived at school and took out the key to my classroom, no squeals could be heard from the other side of the door. Gus' cage was silent. The cinnamon and white fluff ball remained still and curled up in his box of straw. Then, one by one, as the students arrived, they knelt by his cage, whispering their goodbyes, telling Gus how sorry they were. That day, Gus' cage was covered with colorful, hand made thank you cards, expressing gratitude for his friendship; help with reading, his fun, and entertainment. We didn't try to replace Gus with another guinea pig. He was irreplaceable.

16

EEK! A Mouse!

As a pre-school and then a grade-school teacher, I always had a pet snake in the classroom. And that meant I had to have mice to feed the snake. I never kept mice for very long—overnight at the most. Those little beady-eyed, red-eyed white mice from the pet store really stink! Cute as you might regard them, it doesn't matter how often you clean their cages; they reek!

Every month or so, I'd purchase a white mouse at the pet store on my way home from school. Storekeepers handed a mouse to me in a small brown paper bag. As soon as I got to the car, I'd pop the bag with the scrtchy-scratchy sounds coming from inside right into a plastic carrying case. Actually, the hard plastic containers that come in various sizes are meant to be aquariums. They have small slits in the snap-on tops that allow air to circulate.

Once, I'd forgotten to bring the carrying case so I just drove home hurriedly, before the mouse could chew an escape hole in the brown bag. I rushed into the house and immediately transferred the mouse to a lettuce spinner/dryer. Great! The slippery curved sides made it hard for the mouse to climb up. It was a big plastic bowl with a slotted lid on top. Disgusting as it was to put a stinky mouse in a salad bowl, I figured it was a one-time mouse emergency. I planned to sterilize the bowl later and never use it for a rodent container again. I didn't. That darn mouse gnawed a hole in the top and nearly got away before I could get it to school to feed to the snake. I decided to buy a new lettuce spinner/dryer after that. I tossed out the one the mouse wrecked.

I learned my lesson—partially. However, there was another late afternoon that I neglected to put a carrying case in the car. Again, I drove home quickly, thinking, *This time I've got that extra cage in the garage. I'll put the mouse right in that spare cage.* (No more risks with lettuce dryers.)

But, "rats" (pardon the expression) this time the mouse had chewed its way out of the bag *before* I reached our driveway. "Rats," again. "I'll have to make another stop at the pet store tomorrow," I mumbled to myself.

I opened all the doors to the car, front and back, assuming the mouse would run out into the yard sometime in the next few hours, if not before. The mouse would simply have to become a tasty morsel for one of the neighborhood cats instead of necessary food for my snake.

Later, I closed the car doors and put the car in the garage. I drove to school the next day. No mouse. There was no sign of a mouse—no droppings, no scritchy-scratchy sounds—nothing. So I forgot about it.

Months, and I mean months, later, Todd (who was about 17 at the time) asked, "Mom, may I borrow your car to take Sylvia to the prom?"

"Sure." My car was a golden-colored, fairly new Audi. Todd's car was a bright turquoise, sleek, old Pontiac Firebird, and terribly loud—you had to shout over the roar of the powerful engine. It was also a bit unreliable. (It may have been in need of repairs at prom time.) That Firebird was a great car for a teenage surfer kid but not the ideal vehicle for a formal date.

The morning after the prom, I learned that all had not gone well. Taking the Audi to the dance was a big mistake. Todd scowled, "How could you? Why didn't you warn me? I doubt if Sylvia will ever consider going out with me again!"

I was dumbfounded. "What? What did I do? What happened?" I wondered.

"We were driving on the freeway, almost to the dance. Mom, you could have caused a terrible accident."

"Me? I wasn't even there. Was something wrong with my car?" I wanted to know.

"I'll say!" Todd retorted. There was some of your live snake food running around the car, and you never told me!"

"What? What do you mean?" I implored.

Todd explained. "I was driving along. Everything was going well and then suddenly Sylvia screamed—really a loud, piercing shriek that nearly caused me to lose control of the car. A mouse ran over her foot! It had to have been a mouse for your snake! I just know it. And you never told me there was one loose in your car!"

"Oops." I'd forgotten about that escaped mouse. "It was ages ago. I assumed that mouse was long gone. I'm so sorry." I really was. But later, picturing the scene, I had to giggle. It is pretty funny, isn't it?

17

El Ratoncito

We were accustomed to dealing with little field mice in our rented cottage at Estero Beach Resort Hotel in Ensenada, Mexico. The kitchen cottage was at the edge of the wide beach. It backed right up to the sand and dry grasses and scraggly, prickly vines. I always brought mousetraps (and ant traps) with me, to set under the sink and next to the small, slightly dented, slightly rusted-in-spots refrigerator. We brought food with us for a week or two and I needed to protect our supplies from bugs and varmints. (Many items couldn't be purchased in Mexico).

That particular year, when our boys were teenagers, I made sure to bring extra food—feeding teenage boys was one of my specialties! But with all our supplies, somehow I had overlooked the mousetraps—they were nowhere to be found. *No problema.* I'd just go to the office and ask if I could please have a mousetrap or two for our kitchen cottage; I was sure they'd be happy to oblige.

Well, it was not easy to secure a trap. The office at the hotel was jam-packed with freshly arriving guests and no one, at that time, wanted to tend to a problem that an already checked-in guest was having. I simply could not get anyone to take me seriously. "*Si, si, Senora. Mas tarde.*" Later, they would get back to me.

Later, *mas tarde*, no one came to the cottage with a mouse-trap. So when I was sure the office traffic had slowed, I went back. By then, of course, there was no one with authority who could really address my issue; no one knew where the custodians were who might have such a trap. (And, in those days, the resort did not have phones around the premises, not even walkie-talkies. A person, who was not busy, had to hop in a small truck or golf-cart-like contraption and go seek out the particular employee with skills or resources needed.) I left a note for Luis Novelo, one of the resort owners I knew, and went back to our cottage, without a trap in hand.

With all our food and belongings put away, we headed for a spot to perch on the wide stone beach wall to drink in (among other things) a beautiful Mexican red-orange sunset and then went for dinner at the resort's outstanding, equally colorful restaurant. The remainder of the evening was spent playing Scrabble on the front porch of the cottage and our boys, plus friends Tim and Matt, stayed up late with guitars and harmonicas singing their versions of Mariachi music. The boys all slept in their cottage next door until late the next morning, coming into our place for breakfast.

And then all Hell broke loose! "Mom! There's a hole in the cereal box! Cereal crumbs and mouse droppings are everywhere!! And the cracker boxes, too! It looks like mice got into EVERYTHING!! Even the bags of chips are ripped open! How could you *not* have heard all that going on last night?!"

"I don't know. Maybe it all happened when we were at the restaurant. Or out on the porch. Maybe they went away when we came inside." Whenever it was, the mice had done a thorough job, in complete secrecy. There was *not one single package* or bag (bread, bagels, potatoes, apples and oranges included) that did not have at least one hole nibbled in its side. Little bites had been sampled from ALL our food in the cupboards and under the sink. Only canned goods, eggs, meats, milks, cheeses, and vegetables in the refrigerator were spared the mouse invasion. We had eggs and sausages, juice and milk for breakfast.

Mad as could be, I marched up to the office. I took some of the half-shredded boxes as proof. "*Si, si, Senora. Pronto.*" They assured me that someone would be at the cottage "*en un momento.*" With mousetraps.

"En momento"—a minute—became the famous "*manana.*" No one arrived to survey the damage. I got madder and madder as time went on. I began making lists of lost food items, to show the office personnel and for me to use as a replacement-shopping list. I'd have to go into town to see what I could find to substitute for our contaminated food. NOT how I wanted to spend the first day of my vacation! I added "mousetraps" to my shopping list. Still no one from the hotel came to our cottage. So, instead of simply staying there stewing and swearing, I drove into town. It wasn't far away and, I reminded myself, shopping in town was always an entertaining and enterprising adventure.

Bread would be drier than we're used to, melons would be good and fresh, apples and oranges not so much. Bananas are a little different variety than we're used to, but still good. I'd substitute tortillas for sandwich making, and get extra jelly for toast. There would be packaged tortilla chips, I was sure, but getting chips fresh from the hotel restaurant would be even better. I'd manage. But I was still irked at needing to spend the extra time and money to shop for food. An added aggravation was trying to find good, healthy breakfast cereal. No such thing. I had to settle for a box with a familiar Tony the Tiger on the front—sugar frosted flakes—"*Sugaritos*" the label said. It turns out the boys thought that was just fine (and funny), Tim especially. He missed having sugar to put on his cereal. He knew I only offered fruit instead.

I returned from grocery shopping, missing the morning wind-surfing on the bay, which is the best time. (Jeff joked that his mother was the only person he knew who liked to windsurf when there was no wind! He was right—just standing on the board, holding onto the sail and watching the fish swim beneath me or glancing up at clouds and pelicans was heavenly.)

I inquired, "Did anyone come to see the damage and give us some mousetraps?"

"No." No one from the office had come. I felt myself getting upset all over again. I did not put away the food until I'd set mousetraps, each with a bit of peanut butter. No sooner had I done so, than …"SNAP!" came a sound from under the sink! Those little rodents must have been waiting behind the walls for a new supply!

That did it. I reached my limit, no more "nice *Senora*." I did an unforgivable thing. I put all manners and politeness aside. I became an Ugly American, something I'd sworn I'd never be. Armed with the receipt from my shopping in one hand and a tiny dead mouse dangling from a freshly snapped trap in the other, I angrily proceeded to the office. I marched in—newly arriving hotel guests be damned—I used a voice much louder than usual.

"This mouse ruined all our food. I want to be reimbursed. And I want more mousetraps—now! *AHORA!*"

With all eyes on me (or on the dead mouse), tourists and employees gave me immediate attention. I was promised I would not be charged for one night's lodging (more than enough to cover the cost of my groceries) and that I'd find the cleaning staff at my cottage when I returned. I did.

While I was gone, the cleaning lady had discovered yet another mouse caught in a trap I'd set. "Oh, oh," she wailed. "*Pobrecito.*

Pobre ratoncito. Hay muy pequeno." "Poor little mouse. He's so little." And she went on to tell me that he wouldn't have eaten very much. I showed her all the nibbled packages in the trash. "*Lo siento,*" I'm sorry, she said. Sorry for the mouse, or for me?

"*Quien sabe.*" Who knows?

18

El Raton

For years, beginning in the 1970s our family enjoyed vacations at Estero Beach Resort Hotel, just south of Ensenada in Baja California. We spent many holidays there with our boys. That was where Grandpa Jack and I honeymooned with 13 of our combined family members, children and grandchildren, tagging along! Estero Beach still seemed like a luxurious treat in the 1990s, a perfect place to go, especially after days of sandy beach camping with our friends Pam and Kent.

We left our truck in the hotel parking lot at the resort, happy to abandon it for a cool, ocean-view room with a shower and clean sheets on a "real" bed, a relief from tossing and turning in the hot and gritty truck the night before. There I had been awakened numerous times in the dark, unable to identify what creature might possibly have been making all those scrambling around sounds at the base of one of the truck's wheels. It must have been investigating the wheel well closest to where I was trying to sleep. Once or twice I woke up Grandpa to ask him if he heard it…if he thought something was trying to get into the truck.

"No," Grandpa mumbled. "There are lots of nocturnal animals out there…just snooping around, maybe hungry. Our food is secure and they can't get in here." And later, "Don't worry. Go back to sleep. We're all right."

I wasn't. And I did worry. My over-active imagination pictured wild dogs, and large rodents with big, sharp teeth…I could hear claws digging around, really close, I was sure.

At Estero Beach I was back in well lit, clean, nicely furnished, secure surroundings with no threat of invasion. It was a great comfort to feel safe and protected from who-knows-what-kind of critters out there in the wild. I relaxed and slept well after enjoying mariachi music and a delicious non-sandy meal at our favorite restaurant, right at the resort.

We drove home the next day, satisfied that we'd had a great trip: good beach time, camping right near the water, watching the pelicans, pleasure-filled shopping, finding unique curios in the lively Mexican small-town bazaars, a fine visit with old friends, topped off by a perfect stay at our beloved Estero Beach Hotel. Our vacation had included a little bit of everything—an intriguing variety of sights and adventures. We take great pleasure in being able to enjoy all different environments.

And we are always grateful to be able to return home to a place we like equally as well as our get-aways. Driving home from Mexico to Huntington Beach felt like we'd experienced the best of all worlds. (And now we feel that way about Ashland—so fortunate).

Jack began unpacking the truck, to air out sleeping bags, and to hose-off palapas (our canvas awnings). We re-arranged crates with camping gear, straightened out and cleaned our cooking materials. All our dirty clothes got thrown in the washing machine so we'd be prepared for our next adventure, wherever and whenever that would be. We liked to be ready to take a "road trip" at a moment's notice.

"Uh-oh," Grandpa voiced with concern. "Looks like we have a problem." Grandpa showed me one of our "kitchen" crates. The organized, neat stacks of plates, cups, plastic ware and cooking utensils sorted in trays for easy accessibility were no longer visible. The crate was covered with a mass of shredded paper towels!

"Looks like some animal got into the storage area beneath the bed of the truck," Grandpa surmised.

"I *knew* I heard something under my sleeping area the other night!" I insisted.

"Yep. You heard something all right. I'm going to have to unpack everything to make sure we didn't bring a critter home from Mexico."

My imagination took off. "What if we can't find the creature? Then we'll have no idea where it might be. Or what other things it could be destroying! What if I already carried a small beastie into the house with all those items to be washed?

Grandpa tried to calm me. "We'll find out whether it's here, or not!" Grandpa spread tarps across the front lawn. He methodically took out every single crate and carrier bag. Then, piece-by-piece, he removed the custom made carpeted shelving that was part of our camper unit in the back of the truck. All that remained was the empty, metal shell. Still, no stowaway creature appeared. Everything was thoroughly vacuumed and wiped clean—every inch, from the cab to the now empty back of the truck. Nothing unusual was found.

Before nightfall, Grandpa packed everything back into the truck—all tidied and readied for our next trip. "I guess whatever it was must have stayed in Baja," Grandpa announced. "Time for bed."

As we were settling down for the night, Grandpa remembered: "I left my wallet in the glove compartment of the truck. I better go out and get it." He pulled on shorts and T-shirt and, barefooted, padded to the garage.

A few minutes later, Grandpa returned—furious! He seldom swears but he was cursing mightily that night! When he opened the glove compartment door, he was surprised to be faced by a big Mexican beach rat! Evidently the rat was equally surprised; it froze in place and bared its razor-sharp teeth at Grandpa. "Yikes! What did you do?" I asked.

"Slammed the door on the S O B. But I'll get him!" Grandpa stomped back down the hallway to the garage. When he again returned to our bedroom he told me he had set rattraps in the truck. "That'll take care of him." So we went to sleep.

I have no idea how many hours later it was when I became aware that Grandpa had gotten up. His side of the bed was empty. However, it wasn't long before he came back and settled into bed with a satisfied sigh, "Got the S O B!"

19

Cute Kangaroo Rats

Grandpa Jack and I did a lot of camping in Baja California, Mexico. The water on the Sea of Cortez was warm and turquoise and so peaceful. There were often brown pelicans floating by, and fish jumping, as we sat under our palapa out of the direct sun. In the evening, Grandpa put up a windbreak for us, so we continued to sit outside around the fire as the sky darkened and temperatures cooled down. There was still enough light to detect the scurrying around of the little kangaroo rats that made their homes in the rocks by the beach. Occasionally, one of those cute little guys would wander into our campsite.

Campsites in Baja are mostly unadorned—not even picnic tables or a fire pit. But what were present here, much to our delight, were old washing machine tubs. Jack and I have always marveled at Mexican ingenuity. Without a lot of money or resources available for purchase, just about everything a person needed could be fashioned from discarded items. We observed that repairs on cars, houses, roadside stands—you name it— could be made with duct tape, or a combination of duct tape and cardboard or metal scraps or heavy plastic. Very little, except old tires, seemed to go to waste. No, even some of those old tires were cut up to re-sole worn out shoes or make new sandals. And the liners of old washing machine tubs didn't need to be taken to a dump or thrown away. Recycled, they made great fire pits! The inner part of the tub had holes in it, ideal for air circulation to keep a fire alive but retaining ashes and embers that might otherwise be sent flying in the wind.

Our campfire had died down and was out, but still Grandpa and I sat watching the moon's reflection on the water. In the dark, the kangaroo rats became braver. They came quite close, sitting on their tiny haunches, with short "arms" and miniature pink "hands" clasped in front of them. Camel-colored, soft furry coats, they truly do look like little two-to-three inch kangaroos. They peered at us curiously, perhaps hoping for an edible handout.

"Shoo," Grandpa scolded, "go away...scat...get outta here." He kicked a bit of sand in their direction, to send them scattering off. But they weren't discouraged for long and kept creeping back to us.

Before I knew what happened—it was so fast— one made a dangerous dart right across Grandpa's foot. WHOOSH! As I said: it was fast. Grandpa's foot shot up, like a doctor had whapped the reflex point in his knee, and the little rat went flying. PLOP. With a soft thud, the rat landed right smack in the washtub!

"Oh, no," I screamed. "Did it really go into the fire pit?"

"Yep," Grandpa replied. "The fire has been out for a while so I doubt the little guy got burned, but that takes care of one rat."

"Yuck. That's so sad. I'm going to bed," I announced. And I climbed into the truck.

The next morning I still didn't have the heart to poke around the fire pit, fearful of what I might discover. I don't know if the kangaroo rat survived its rocket flight and crash-landing, or not. However, kangaroo rats can leap as far as seven feet, so I like to assume the little rat leapt out of the washing machine tub later that night, after Jack, "the kicker," had gone to sleep.

20

Templeton

Lots of people's pet rats are named Templeton…after the notorious rat in E. B. White's book, *Charlotte's Web*. "Templeton" was what my pre-school students insisted we call our school's new baby rat.

Templeton, at Hilltop Preschool in Costa Mesa, California, was adored year after year by numerous classes of 3, 4, and 5-year olds who entered and then graduated to go on to elementary school. Scores of former students came back to visit Templeton (and Queenie, the King Snake) at every Open House and school event for alumni.

Templeton spent more time out of his cage than in it. He sat on children's laps at story time and, if a parent/teacher was free and available to supervise, Templeton was again allowed out of his cage, for no reason other than to be cuddled and loved.

Families at the preschool added their names to a long waiting list, hoping to be the lucky ones to take Templeton home for a weekend or vacation time. (That was lucky for me, too. Usually

I had to cart home only the toads. Most parents didn't want to help take care of muddy, warty toads with their incessant need to be fed live, wiggly mealworms.)

Templeton *never* bit anyone, contrary to some assumptions about rats. There is a HUGE difference between pet "lab" rats and rats that live in the wild. It's like the difference between pet dogs and wild wolves. Templeton came when he was called. He endured squeezing little hands. Sometimes I was sure I even saw his eyes bulge a little when preschoolers grasped him tightly around the middle! Still, no matter what the torture, he never bit—just squirmed uncomfortably now and then. Templeton liked to nuzzle into children's laps or tickle at their necks, trying to get under and hide in long hair if it hung down low enough. He was affectionate and exceptionally clean and sweet smelling, again contrary to what some people expect of rats.

One year, when Templeton was ancient, well beyond a usual life expectancy of 5 years for rats, he went home for the summer with the Gable family. Templeton waddled along uncertainly. He'd either lost his hearing or his bearing at that point. In any case he no longer came when called. Perhaps it was stubborn independence or just being obstinate that accompanies both 2-year-old and 92-year-old behavior. But the Gable family knew about Templeton's shortcomings in old age—their children had been in the school for years, certainly as long as Templeton. They didn't mind that he slept a lot or that his fur was thinning in spots and a bit uneven.

They knew that Templeton was likely spending his last days with them that summer. And they consoled themselves that, if he died, he would die happy.

And, boy, was he happy!! The Gables let Templeton wander freely in their shady backyard, watching him carefully as he waddled and wavered through their nice, green grass. Templeton, they said, found a favorite place under their peach tree. It was a long trip across the lawn, but he insisted on making the trip each day. He nibbled quite contentedly on the peaches that dropped from the tree. However, as the summer wore on, Templeton became wobblier than ever. He got more roly-poly, sometimes even tumbling over on one side and having difficulty righting himself again. It was John, the Gable kids' dad, who observed that Templeton appeared to be inebriated. (In other words, John thought that Templeton walked like he was drunk.) It turned out that as the peaches became over-ripe and fell to the ground, they quickly rotted in the summer heat. John sniffed one and said it smelled "fermented." It seemed the natural sugars in the fruit, as it decayed, were slowly turning the peach juice into alcohol—like a peach wine or rum!! Templeton was indeed drunk...extremely intoxicated on fermented peaches!! He died at the end of summer, John said, "With a happy smile on his face...feeling no pain."

21

The Critters Behind The Stove

In 1980, our family lived in the country of Bahrain, on the Arabian Gulf, in the Middle East. We lived at one end of the expatriate neighborhood of A'Ali, surrounded by miles of flat sand, except for the ancient grave mounds that gave the impression of smooth, slightly rising sand dunes. No vegetation to be seen; just a few plants in our own yard. We were about a 20-minute drive from the city of Manama, Bahrain.

Our kitchen was tiny so it wasn't surprising that I could hear barely detectable scratchy sounds coming from behind the small propane gas stove. Standing at the sink, looking out the window onto the beige Bahraini desert, I could reach the small British-made washing machine in the corner to my right and the stove next to that. I could extend my left arm to touch the shoulder-high refrigerator.

Washing dishes one evening after dinner (there was no dishwasher) I was alerted by some little squeaks. *Oh, no. Somehow a mouse got in here*, I thought. I called for my teenage sons and my husband. "Do you hear that?" They did. My husband set a mousetrap and placed it in the corner next to the stove, back against the kitchen wall.

Next morning, sure enough, I spied a dark grey, charcoal-colored, furry body in the trap. Using the broom, I pulled the trap toward me. It **wasn't** a mouse! It was bigger than a mouse, but not rat size. And the face! Again, I yelled for the boys. We stood and stared down at the unusual little critter. It had a pointed, protruding nose, pinkish, and funnel-like. "Is that a mole?" I wondered out loud.

We had no means for researching rodents. We could only guess. On closer examination, we did discover that the animal, dead in the trap, was a nursing mother. Swollen pink teats were plainly visible.

"Oooh," I groaned. "That means those squeaks I heard were babies! There must be babies under the stove!"

Ever so carefully, my husband and my two sons, crowded in the corner of the kitchen, inched the stove away from the wall. And, there, in a nest of sorts (perhaps made of a shredded paper napkin) were inch-long, pink and gray, oval-shaped, squirming bodies—three of them—like fat, wrinkled jelly beans, eyes shut tight, all with pointed pink noses.

"How will I ever save them?" My thoughts were rushing. Words tumbled out. "Who can I call for advice? It's Saturday. No offices will be open—it's the Sabbath. ...I know. I'll call Faisal and Haifa."

Faisal was the Director of Al Areen, Bahrain's desert museum; his wife, Haifa, was my good friend, both from Lebanon. Faisal had fashioned Al Areen after the Desert Wildlife Museum in Tucson, Arizona, which he'd visited and had been impressed by years before. The Museum was devoted to caring for and protecting wild, native species.[17]

Faisal, as I'd hoped, offered immediate assistance, instructing me to keep the mole babies warm. (From my description he said it was likely that we did, indeed, have little moles; they live all over Asia, North and South America.)

I lined a shoebox with washcloths, put the babies in and placed the box in the closet that contained the hot water heater. I put the shoebox on the floor, near the pilot light. It was warmer there, and dark and quiet… "usual conditions for moles," Faisal said.

He told me that he'd alert the staff at Al Areen and someone would meet me at the gates that afternoon. In the meantime, I was to keep the babies warm and try to give them a few drops of warm water—no telling how many hours they'd gone without nourishment. I had an eyedropper and gave each little mole a tiny amount of liquid.

With the heater on in the car, I drove across the desert. A young man and woman were waiting for me at the gates to Al Areen. They peeked in my covered shoebox. "Yes, moles, very young," they said.

"May I call you every day or so to find out how they are doing?" I asked.

"Of course. But they're only a day or so old. They may not survive…we will do what we can. *En sha' Allah.*" God willing.

I thanked them and drove home. The next day I learned that one had died.

As days went on, the two survivors did well and I was told

17 Al Areen had just opened in 1976, so it was brand new then. Now, more than 40 years later, the videos shown on the Internet are very much like Arizona's Wildlife Museum—a large, impressive tourist attraction. In 1980, it was simply a small compound surrounded by chain link fencing.

they would be released in the desert once they were older and able to thrive on their own.

What a relief it was to know that I had not wiped out an entire family of little critters. It seems that moles in Bahrain must not be very common, or even still existing in Bahrain, as they are no longer on the country's list of mammals or rodents. I'm glad I did what I could to save them.

22

Befriending A Wild Saluki in Bahrain

When our family lived in the Middle East in the country of Bahrain for the year of 1980, we learned about critters we'd never encountered before. During that year, my son Todd was a lovesick teenager, determined to profess his love to the universe. He confessed years later that he wandered out into the desert around our home in the middle of the night, on several occasions, to construct a monument to his love. He gathered rocks in the moonlight, and placed them so they could be read from the heavens above: "A-n-a-b-e-l-a."[18]

While landscaping with rocks in the desert, Todd felt the presence of animals but didn't see them at first. And that's understandable. Salukis are wild dogs of the Middle East, many of them the color of the desert, and are known to be standoffish, aloof and wary of strangers, even after they've been tamed or brought up as pups by human beings. The Salukis that watched

---

18 Anabela was from Portugal, where she and her family now live. She and Todd remain friends and are still in touch. We all are. We all have memories of the romance of living in beautiful Bahrain.

Todd evidently became more and more curious and must not have felt threatened by the lad who worked silently and thoughtfully in the night. They gradually came closer and closer to him. He spotted them out of the corner of his eye, paused now and then to speak quietly to the dogs, but was not able to convince any to come within petting distance. He told me that he took pieces of bread and dinner leftovers out to them. Finally, a few braver members of the pack would dart in closer to him to snatch food morsels from his hand, and then quickly retreat.

"Oh, so that's how the young Saluki came to be at our door-step," I pondered.

"Yes," Todd admitted. It had followed him home from one of his evening outings. Our house was way out in the desert. We were situated on a corner lot, without any other houses on two sides. Those sides were open to the vast desert; low rolling sand dunes as far as you could see. And it was from there that we often heard the strange coyote-like howls at night. The sounds were lower pitched than those of our American southwestern coyotes, and more staccato, but not yipping—just short, rapid-fire, deeper barks, alternating with whining cries or howls, again, in a lower range than we recognized. Now that Todd had lured one of the dogs to our doorstep, we knew the source of those nighttime serenades.

Our Bahraini friends warned us, "Those dogs are wild. Be careful." They didn't know of anyone who kept a Saluki as a pet. But we missed our dog from back home. Our Labrador retriever, Bob, had been kenneled (happily on a farm in Orange County, California) for the year we lived in the Middle East. We'd always had lots of pets; we enjoyed having them around.

We invited that Saluki into our Bahrain desert home but he always refused. He came to visit us every evening; he ate the food we left on the porch for him and drank the water, but we were never able to coax him to come inside and he never let us touch him.

Now, researching Salukis of the Middle East, we see that they are domesticated, considered to be among the oldest and best breeds of hunting dogs and certainly the fastest dogs on the planet. Salukis can run nearly 43 miles per hour! They are similar-looking to greyhounds; both sleek animals are bred for racing. Salukis have paws that are adapted to high-speed runs in the desert sand. They have webbing between their toes that prevents them from sinking, much like the way snowshoes work for us in soft snow.

Years later, we can still clearly picture the large, warm, inquisitive eyes, and floppy ears of that sweet, light gold colored, slim dog that came to see us, but kept its distance the whole year we lived in the Middle East. I wonder how long he continued to come to the house after we had gone. I do know, that with the Saluki's reputation for hunting, for needing little water, and for being able to run for long periods of time for great distances, he surely was never hungry or in need, unless it was for some human connection. I wonder.

23

The Raccoon Family Circus

Before our contractor, "Ben the Builder," told us to stop feeding the birds, our backyard provided daily (and nightly) wildlife entertainment. The birds were abundant: quail, towhee, flickers, and woodpeckers among my favorites. Our back gate opens directly into North Mountain Park, at the top of the grassy hill that has the last of Ashland's old white oak trees, home to all sorts of creatures. Among the animals that came for the birdseed, were rats and mice, naturally. So much so that Ben discovered a rat infestation beneath our house! Yuck! That was disgusting, and the reason why we followed Ben's advice. But before we got rid of the feeders, we had visits from deer, squirrels, raccoons and an occasional fox, skunk, and opossum...all attracted by the birdseed.

The raccoons were the funniest. They were the clowns in our backyard circus. We spent many hours sitting and looking out our wall of windows, with Grizzly Peak in the background, watching the show. Roly-poly raccoons tumbled over one another in their eagerness to devour the peanuts which had dropped to the ground. They scrambled in the dirt, and balanced and trotted along the low fence, though a bit wobbly at times. Sometimes the bravest one crept onto the deck that adjoins the house and, with its robber-like masked face, it peered in right through the dining room French doors!

"Come, watch this," Grandpa Jack beckoned one evening. A big, fat mama raccoon and her three chubby little babies were nosing around, exploring the whole yard. One baby began climbing the trellis that forms a high arch over the back gate. Dangling from the top of the arch was a water dish for the birds, one of those that hang from three small chains supporting it and keeping it balanced.

Soon the other little raccoons followed suit, all ascending the trellis, with eyes on that water dish, curious about what it might contain. Mama raccoon was oblivious. She concentrated on morsels on the ground below the arch and didn't even glance at her babies. She seemed totally absorbed and unaware of what her youngsters were up to.

"Oh, no." We could see it coming. We held hands and held our breaths, waiting for the inevitable. Can *you* imagine what was about to happen?

It seemed to take forever, unfolding in slow motion. One baby reached the top of the trellis. He peered down into the water dish. The other two followed. One of their feet slipped through the wood slats, throwing a plump raccoon off-balance. We gasped. He was okay.

All three slipped and swayed up there on top of the rounded arch. Then, one lay down on top and stretched a paw between the slats, reaching toward the water dish. He couldn't touch it. The other raccoons tried, too. Mama raccoon kept right on eating, still totally unaware of her babies messing around right above her head! We watched and waited with bated breaths. And then it happened!

A baby raccoon grasped one of the small chains attached to the water dish, attempting to draw it closer. Yikes! The dish wobbled a bit—then tilted—oops. And SPLASH! Nearly a quart of water dumped directly down, all over the unsuspecting mama raccoon!

No more slow-motion disaster about to unfold. Everything sped up. Mama raccoon jumped with surprise, jerked her head up, and glared. Three baby raccoons, eyes wide and frightened looking, one after the other, tumbled down the side of that trellis, close to falling numerous times. They were not pausing to test their footing, but getting out of there as fast as they possibly could! They hit the ground, running, racing around the side of the house, out of sight from us. Mama raccoon followed in quick pursuit...there must have been a terrific scolding and batting around after that. We still laugh just thinking about that circus act.

24

Rats in the Attic: Good News and Bad News

As I mentioned, our backyard opens up to the field and old oak grove at the top of North Mountain Park. It's not surprising that we get lots of critters visiting us from the adjoining nature park. Field mice and rats are frequent invaders.

Grandpa Jack puts rattraps in the attic of our garage and checks them regularly. Since we've stopped storing birdseed in the garage, there is less to attract rodents. Still, in cold weather, the warm attic is quite welcoming, I'm sure. And when it's hot outside, the dark, shady garage offers respite from the glaring sun.

Grandpa Jack baits the rattraps with peanut butter. He has to climb up the tall ladder, move aside the overhead plywood door, reach in for the switch, and turn on the light. Then he climbs further up the ladder to peer inside the attic. His body is actually in the attic, from head to hips, while his feet remain firmly on one of the top rungs of the ladder.

After one of Grandpa's routine checks, he came back down the ladder and into the kitchen to announce: "Well, I have good news and I have bad news." He asked, "Which do you want to hear first?"

"I always prefer good news," I reminded him.

"O.K. I caught a rat. That's the good news. The bad news is that I couldn't find him. Finally, after much searching around, I spotted him. But there's more bad news: I can't reach him."

"How could that be?"

Grandpa Jack explained. Evidently when the trap snapped, the rat must have struggled to escape. Somehow, he managed to drag the trap across the floor of the attic to the edge where the heater ducts come through. The rat, with the trap attached to him, fell down into the space below the attic floor and above the ceiling of the rooms in the house—into that in-between space for insulation and heating/air conditioning ducts.

"I can see him down there but I can't get him out."

"Does that mean the dead rat will just have to stay there and rot? That could smell terrible for a long time! Is there someone we can call?"

Grandpa Jack muttered: "I'll figure out a way. I'll take care of it."

He always does. However, it took a long time. Finally, with an unbent, straightened-out wire coat hanger, Grandpa was able to reach down, snag, and fish out the trap with the dead rat.

Whew!

P.S. When I read this story to Grandpa Jack to check for accuracy, he said, "Yep. That's what happened."

I quizzed him some more. "It's a short story. But I think it's a funny one. Don't you?"

"No. I don't think it's funny," he replied. "That incident was frustrating and required a lot of time and effort."

I'm including the story anyway. In spite of Grandpa's lack of enthusiasm, I am hoping that you find it as amusing as I do.

25

A Baby By the Road

Just the other morning I walked through North Mountain Park, up Mountain Avenue, past the retirement community, to the freeway. It wasn't too hot yet so I decided to cross the freeway over-ramp to Nevada Street. I turned right to the horse and cattle farms up there.

First I came to a bunch of goats. About twenty, of all sizes, were grazing on the dried weeds and grasses. As I passed their fenced in, enclosed pasture area, I waved to a lady who was walking through a big iron gate, up the driveway through the goat farm. Next, I walked by about half a dozen cows, crowded under a tree in the shade. "Good idea," I told them, "it's getting warm already." I went on talking, telling them how wise they were to find a place out of the now blazing sun. They all watched me, expressionless, but I was sure they agreed...even the little calf. None of them moved one bit; only their eyes lazily tracked my progress down the road.

Along my way, I kept picking up aluminum cans and finally retrieved an old black plastic trash bag from the blackberry bushes. I dumped my armload of smashed cans in the bag and continued to add another one here and there.

After I'd gone about two miles, past the horse farms, I turned around. I passed by those cows again; they still hadn't moved an inch. I spoke to them again. They seemed totally disinterested. Then I came to the goats. They were a bit livelier, some still munching but a few were butting heads, and one was leaping around. They "baa-baa-ed" at me so I "baa-baa-ed" back at them. Movement in the grasses near to me caught my attention. I stopped to peek through the dry brush and spotted a really small white baby goat on MY side of the fence! It was only about eight feet from the road.

I stood to watch the cute fuzzy little thing crunching away at the star thistle—ugh—and I told it, "You shouldn't be out here. You belong inside the fence with all the other goats." It paused to look up at me and then went back to eating weeds. I said, "Come with me, Little Goat. We'll find a way to get you back inside the fence." It came a bit closer to me, still munching. "C'mon, c'mon," I urged the baby. It kept coming. I wondered, *should I reach out for its small, 2-inch, horns to lead it back up the road? No*, I thought, *I won't be able to get a good hold*. I continued to call the goat toward me and when it was right up close, I bent over and scooped it into my arms, one arm under its chest and one arm under the rump.

I'd guess the goat was about two feet in length and about 18 inches high but solid, and sturdier than I imagined—maybe 15 pounds or so. It nestled comfortably against me. I held it to my chest and began walking back toward the gate to the goat farm. The baby goat tried to nibble the black plastic trash bag I was carrying. "No, no. That wouldn't be good for you." I moved the bag more to my side so, even when the goat craned its neck around, it couldn't reach the bag. Then it tried nibbling on my shirt. "No, no, not that either," I told it. The baby goat wriggled a little, a feeble attempt to escape, I think, but then it relaxed and settled back into my arms.

I was getting tired carrying that goat uphill (uphill tires me anyway.) But I couldn't find an opening in the fence. The fence was about 5 feet tall, eye level, with a string of barbed wire stretched across the top. I knew I couldn't lift the baby goat up and over my head, and then over the fence without scraping it or me on the barbed wire. And I certainly didn't want to drop it down from that height!

Arms aching, getting out of breath, I kept walking. Cars went by but no one stopped or even slowed down to help an old lady in a big hat, carrying a trash bag and a baby goat. Finally, I made it to the metal gate. It was no longer open but closed securely with a big padlock and chain. The lady goat farmer was nowhere in sight. Her truck was gone. The golden retriever sheep dog (or should I say goat dog?) was barking like crazy, but there was no one around. The dog was locked inside an enclosure near its doghouse at the other end of the driveway.

What to do? I decided to try to fit the goat between the metal bars on the gate. That wouldn't get it back inside the fenced pasture with the other goats, but it would be away from the road and at least onto the farm property. I dropped my trash bag and leaned over, tilting the baby goat away from my body; our torsos were at right angles, with its legs sticking out on either side of my waist. I gently lowered its head through the bars, then shoulders and rump. I wiggled it a bit to get its legs through and dropped it ever so gently to the ground. It was only about a foot off the ground at that point and it landed on all four feet and gave a little spring toward the greenery along the side of the driveway that led to the barn. It just stayed there, nibbling on milkweed, and ignored me.

I supposed the baby goat could squeeze back out through the gate to the road again, but I believed I left it in a safer place for the time being. Hopefully the farmer would return soon to round up all the goats and would notice the baby when she unlocked the big gate.

I picked up my trash bag and continued home, still with warm feelings left by the baby goat pressed against my chest and the inward glow that comes from having done a good deed.

***

And here I thought I was finished with critters—having raised them and rescued them (avoiding only a few) all my life—and darned if that baby goat didn't appear at the side of the road, irresistible. It just goes to show, as my grandma used to say, "You're not done yet, kid." So keep your eyes and ears, and your heart open. The possibilities of connecting with critters of all kinds, even human ones, are always there.

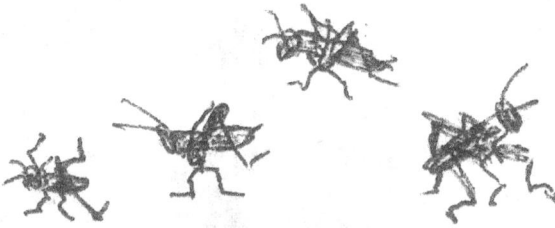

The End

for now...

About the Author

Lynn Ransford was born in Los Angeles, California, and moved with her family from the city to a chicken farm in the San Fernando Valley, where she grew up surrounded by a variety of animals. A little like Beverly Cleary's *Ramona*, or L.M. Montgomery's *Anne of Green Gables*, Lynn often got into bits of trouble.

Years later she married Grandpa Jack, a mountaineer, who introduced her to animals in the wild and some wild adventures. Grandpa adds, "She still gets herself into a little trouble occasionally." Their ten grandchildren find stories of those times entertaining, most of all when they encountered critters!

Lynn has a Master's degree in Education, three lifetime credentials, and is an Early Childhood Specialist. She recently earned her Naturalist Certificate from Siskiyou Field Institute in Selma, Oregon, and has written numerous grants in the field of education: articles, curricula, creative teaching materials and books for teachers.

Lynn co-authors the scripts for her docent work at the Historic Beekman House in Jacksonville, Oregon, and for Living History programs offered at historic cemeteries in both Ashland and Jacksonville. Lynn says, "dressing up" in period costumes for the roles of Oregon pioneers is "a lot of fun." She also enjoys hiking, camping, quilting, writing memoirs and poetry.

Now a retired teacher after 50 years in pre-school through University/Graduate level classrooms, Lynn writes the stories her students loved and the ones the grandchildren want to hear over and over. She has discovered that friends of all ages enjoy listening to these sometimes funny, sometimes scary, or sometimes poignant, true tales.

Acknowledgements

First of all I must thank my family for their support, encouragement, and tolerance with me throughout the process of writing
Grandma, Tell Me A Story…".

My grandchildren asked again and again, "Grandma, tell me
a story…". They got me started. Then my niece and nephew asked
for more. My sons humored me in my storytelling. Sometimes
they corrected me: "Mom, that's not really what happened; you
must have imagined that."

My brother Mike stood up for me. (He always did.) "It's her
story. That's her perception so it's real to her." Sometimes my
sons added to the storytelling, embellishing family tales with
details I didn't remember, or confessions they hadn't admitted
in their youth.

Deciding whether or not to publish my stories, my younger
brother and sister said, "Go for it. I think you should do it." My
brother Tom added a warm, teasing joke that I appreciated: "Who
knows? Maybe you'll be famous one day."

That was not the intent. My wish was to preserve our favorite family stories for grandchildren. I planned to have the local
printer run-off and spiral bind about fifteen copies.

"Don't," insisted my already published, historian friend, Sue
Waldron. "Before you have the printer put your stories together,
you must see Ginna and David Gordon of Lucky Valley Press, in

Jacksonville." That advice from Sue turned out to be a blessing for which I'm truly thankful.

Ginna and David, both extremely talented and successful in numerous artistic endeavors, are devoted to helping and encouraging artists and authors to publish their works. Using IngramSpark as their preferred printer and distributor, Ginna and David agreed to assist me with publishing (something I knew I'd never be able to do on my own). *Grandma…* stories then could be widely available to others beyond our family. They predicted that, besides grandchildren, adults would be entertained by stories of animals in the wild…anyone who had also experienced encounters with "critters" or anyone who *wished* they had. Ginna and David created endearing book covers to package the stories—far beyond my original vision of plain ol' spiral bound copies.

My friend Sue also insisted that I make some simple little drawings to go with each story: "Just small, one- or two-inch doodles to catch the eye." That was easy for her to say. Like Ginna and David, Sue is an artist. And so is another good friend, Suzanne Marshall. Suzanne marched right over to my house, arms loaded with sketchbooks and how-to-draw books. "You can do it!"

I got out my old Irene Brady Nature Sketching journals from classes I'd taken with her at Siskiyou Field Institute years ago. Working on the small sketches turned out to be almost as much fun as the writing!

And Suzanne Marshall did more. She became my unofficial agent, organizing a book-signing party in the midst of COVID-19 pandemic concerns. "We'll have a porch signing party…each guest who buys a book will also get a mug of hot apple cider and a cookie." Everyone came! What fun that was!

My bi-monthly writing group must be acknowledged also. Udo Gorsch-Nies, Lizzie McDermott, and Susanne Krieg gave me positive feedback and constructive suggestions to improve my stories. And, Carol Moore, who left our writing group in Ashland to move to Eugene, continued to send me input by email. "I enjoy reading your stories and I don't mind editing them." WOW! Carol is an experienced writer/editor and so expert at spotting grammar, syntax, punctuation, and needs for clarification. I am deeply indebted to her for her time, expertise, and gentle suggestions for fixing stories, readying them for printing.

I also apreciate the time and editing skills of my three good friends Connie Crow, Sue Blaize, and Marian Crumme, who generously gave up precious vacation hours to help me with corrections.

***

My dear husband, who appears in numerous chapters of the book, as "Grandpa Jack," was the deciding factor in my decision to publish our family stories. I hesitated at the cost of publication and, without giving it further thought, Jack laughed and admitted, "One of my fly rods costs more than that." He went on: "You spend that much on our grandchildren at holiday times—think of the stories as gifts to our children and grandchildren."

What a gift Jack has been to me! In so many ways—he is to be commended for his patience, his humor, his honesty, and providing me with great, first-hand material for stories!

***

Thank you to everyone for your help and contributions, for your love and encouragement. I am forever grateful.